Garrett Lee Murray

Extreme Survival
Pocket Guide

By Garrett Lee Murray

COPYRIGHT © 2011

I dedicate this guide to my children: Jacob, Devon, and Jessica Murray. I hope this guide helps you through life after I am gone. Know that I love you all and hope that your life struggles are minimal.

Disclaimer

By reading this guide you acknowledge that you take full responsibility for your actions. The information provide within this guide is for educational purposes only and should only be tested in extreme situations. Any illegal activities or harm brought onto others is completely your responsibility and I take no responsibility for anything that happens. I also take no responsibility for misinformation within this guide that might possibly cause injury or death. The information has been tested in the field and has worked for me and other survivalists and should work for you if done properly.

Kids should be supervised at all times when attempting anything written in this book. Use extreme caution when attempting any of these activities.

Introduction

Survival

noun
1: a state of surviving; remaining alive.
2: a natural process resulting in the evolution of organisms' best adapted to the environment.
3: something that survives.

Welcome to the Extreme Survival Pocket Guide, to surviving extreme disasters. We all know no one can really predict the future so we need to prepare for anything. This guide is about the most extreme circumstances and the things I talk about in this guide should only be considered in the most extreme cases like, "the fall of our Government". In this guide I will explain what you will need and where you can find it if you don't have it already. Understand this is only a guide and not a complete handbook to safety. Please seek more knowledge, look for books written for the military. Scout, SAS, Survival FM's and handbooks are great material to learn from. The setting for this guide would be in the North American cities and woodland environments. These are more common areas people reside in.

When you think of surviving you should think of term **<u>SURVIVAL</u>**:

S Size up the situation (Survey your surroundings, physical condition, and equipment on hand).

U Use your senses (Hear, see, feel, taste, smell and sense).

R Remember where you are (City, woods, or desert).

V Vanquish fear and panic (Stay calm).

I Improvise when possible (hammer as a weapon)

V Value life (Want to survive)

A Act like the Natives (Animals, birds, and local people).

L Live by using common sense but for now learn the basics (Instincts).

Index

Turn the page if you want to survive!

Chapter 1

What to prepare for

Natural Disasters come in many different forms hurricanes, earthquakes, floods, volcanoes, meteor collision, droughts, or even windstorms. Even manmade disasters can be just as destructive as natural disasters, such as riots, genocide, nuclear war, chemical warfare, or world wars. Preparing for them is going to be key to your survival.

Make a list, make sure everything you pack is sealed in Ziploc bags and in a plastic bin (bin should be water proof and be able to float). Overloading your bin may cause the bin not to float. Don't place all your items in one location. Placing all your items in one location leaves you at risk of losing everything in a disaster. Look at getting storage units, bury things in different locations, or even have an RV packed and ready to go if possible.

Have a disaster plan in place to be prepared. Make sure that everyone in your family is aware of the plans. If your home is destroyed, no longer safe or if separated at the time of a disaster, you should have a rally point (rally point is a designated place everyone goes to in case they are separated). Have multiple rally points in case one is compromised. Each plan should be labeled as A, B and C and followed in order if the last plan is compromised. Try to make sure that everyone in the family has a roll in the disaster plan that you have put in place. This will make it easier and it will show responsibility on everyone's part.

  Practice the emergency plan. Just like fire drills at school or work you should practice drills at home or wherever you are at. If you are on the road, have the person driving take an alternate route home. Act as if the road is damaged or the route is blocked. See if you can navigate by a map, not GPS. In an extreme disaster, such as a possible poll shift (predicted by scientist that this has happened in the past and will happen again) GPS may be disabled and even compasses may become inaccurate. That is why it's important to practice now. Knowing more than one route home from work, school, or even the grocery store will prove to be beneficial in many different scenarios.

  Don't wait until the last minute to get your list around. It may get too hard to find the time to do everything and with panic setting in finding some items may be a bigger challenge at the last minute. Start with the basics: medical, food, clothing, water, and gas. Then think about: weapons, ammunition, generators, survival gear, rafts, and even larger items like a boat and motor home. Do little things at a time. Purchase a couple of cans of spam when you are out each time at the store. Spam's shelf life is almost as long as MRE's making this a great alternative if you can't afford MRE's. There are many recipes for Spam on the internet that you might want to get familiar with.

In case of flooding situations, you will need a boat or life raft to survive. Have one at the ready with clean water and food. Fishing supplies would be handy too. If you have to move do to fires, floods, or whatever you will need a vehicle and a tent. Consider a motor home or camper, these can hold everything you need and offer better protection from the elements than a tent could. Only down side to a motor home is that it can eat up the gas in no time and its size makes it difficult to maneuver in tight situations. If you run into a situation that roads are partially blocked being in an oversized vehicle might cause more headaches than it may be worth.

Bug out Bag

A bug out bag is a bag that has everything you need to survive for 72 hours. You could purchase them online or you can make your own. I find it better to make your own because I don't believe one size fits all. Everyone in the family should have one of these bags. If you create one for the kids, add some toys to keep them from getting bored.

The properly made bug-out bag should contain enough supplies to last at least 72 hours. Some bug out bags include small survival rehydration bags (small sealed bags of water), but I think having the means to make clean water is just as important if not more. A good bug-out kit includes:

- ➤ Survival Food high in fats, (Spam) carbs and calories for the energy you will need.
- ➤ Clothing, including rain gear and proper footwear. Functionality and warmth are priority.
- ➤ Shelter materials. For example: a tarp, small tent or Bivy bag. You should also include a light weight sleeping bag.
- ➤ Water and means to purify water.
- ➤ First-aid materials.
- ➤ Basic survival gear such as a good knife and Paracord.
- ➤ Ability to make a fire by at least three means. For example: waterproof matches, FireSteel, magnifying glass, and lighter.
- ➤ Hygiene kit
- ➤ Map
- ➤ Cards for entertainment.
- ➤ Survival radio (something that doesn't rely on just batteries).
- ➤ Compass
- ➤ Solar blanket

> Small amount of cash

I would add a knife, gun and ammunition. These things you would not be able to purchase with a B.O.B.

Food should have a long shelf life. MRE's, (Meals Ready to Eat) are perfect for long storage. Normally a MRE contains high fat and protein items with a main custom meal, fruit and desert. Along with that they also carry other items such as: matches, toilet paper, a heater to warm your food, small container of Tabasco sauce, salt, pepper, coffee, creamer, sugar and plastic ware. Each MRE contains around 1200 calories just enough to sustain you in the wilderness. I normally found the MRE to have more than enough to eat from for an entire day. Typically a body needs about 1200 calories per day to survive on as long as you aren't that active.

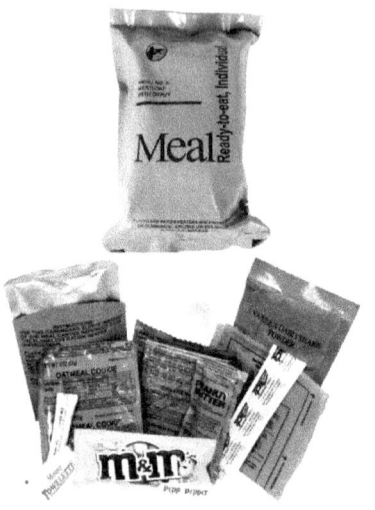

Knowing your battles

When natural disasters happen and the government doesn't respond timely expect crime to go way up. Have a weapon or two at hand and the know how to use them. Two or more magazines should be filled with the proper ammunition and carried on you at all times. Additional magazines are suggested just in case you are in a fire fight and you don't want to be stuck reloading. In the U.S. Army I carried 8 magazines on me at all times filled with 30 rounds each. Really that isn't much in a fire fight and can be expended quickly.

It's also important to know what ammunition to use. In the Military they use FMJ, (Full Metal

Jackets). This is typically great ammunition to use when training because it's inexpensive and does some damage to the target. Only down side to FMJ is that it's considered training ammunition because it can hit a target and continue right through it making it a danger for what may be beyond the target. Back in the day when they use to fight wars away from civilians and each side wore war uniforms to distinguish them apart from civilians it wasn't bad to use FMJ. Two with one shot was even better but today's wars are fought in cities with civilians all around. We need to make sure our rounds hit and stay in the intended target.

The better ammunition to have is hollow points they break or fragment into pieces in your intended target and are less likely to come out the other side. Larger caliber ammunition is also better for keeping the round in the intended target. Basically smaller ammunition goes through more but causes less damage. Larger ammunition will penetrate less but leaves a bigger hole. Bigger the opening the more blood that comes out and that person will be less likely to live.

Pick your battles, "there is nothing wrong with running". If you feel like you might be out gunned run and fight another day. This isn't the movies and you are not Rambo, (if you are Rambo you don't need this manual). You aren't going to survive a fight against a platoon of men by yourself. The best fight is not fighting at all. Hide, observe, and move around. If you have no other option take well aimed shots. It's not a competition to see who can put more lead down range. Ammunition is not cheap especially if you are using hollow points. Consider finding the best cover and concealment before engaging your target. Allow for an escape route if you are unable to successfully scare off or kill the enemy.

Use the right weapon when engaging the target. Why go in blasting people away with a fully automatic rifle when the guy only had a knife? Size it up, if the target has a knife use a bow, (if unseen) or a hand gun. If the target has a handgun and you have a distance advantage use a long range rifle, (one shot one kill). I personally believe you should have multiple weapons for different scenarios. I recommend a 12 gauge for hunting, (within 200 yards) small arms rifle, (for longer shots) and two hand guns of different caliber, (one for backup if other fails). Also consider knifes, bow and crossbows to conserve ammunition to when you really need it.

Time to pack up

Besides having a Bug-Out-Bag you should have additional supplies packed up and ready to go.

The large totes used to store stuff in your shed or storage unit are great for packing these supplies in. Here is a sample packing list for you to go off of.

Sample packing list (Long term supplies)

Medical: (Hospitals, Rite-Aid, Walgreens)

- ➢ Medication (understand these expire so date your container and replace as needed).
  - o Aspirin
  - o Flu medication
  - o Motrin
  - o Tylenol
  - o Other personal medication
- ➢ Bandages
- ➢ Soap
- ➢ IV bags
- ➢ Surgical tools
- ➢ Dental hygiene
- ➢ Alcohol
- ➢ Peroxide
- ➢ Sting/bite kits
- ➢ Surgical Tape
- ➢ Butterfly Bandages/ Steri strips

Food: (Army Navy surplus store carries MRE's)

- ➢ Spam
- ➢ Beans
- ➢ Rice

- Dried Fruits
- Can goods
- Powder Milk
- Salt
- Sugar
- Other spices
- Jerky (optional, may spoil)

Clothing: (weeks' worth)

- Underwear
- Socks
- Shirts
- Cold Weather Jacket
- Gloves
- Face mask
- Hat
- Sun Glasses
- Boots (thick sole)
- Blankets
- Towel
- Wash cloth
- Pants (camo is best or denim)

Water: (water towers, tap from wells only, running streams, vending machines and grocery stores)

- Store as much as you can, cache a lot in different locations.
- Water purification system is a must (Look into a UV light purifier).

Gas: gas stations, bus garage, farms, large corporations, or public works.

- ➢ 10 - 5 gallon cans of gas, mixed with stabilizer treatment.
- ➢ Oil preferably the type your vehicle needs.
- ➢ Oil for engines that use a mix (boats, chainsaws or two stroke engines).
- ➢ Keep vehicle topped off (nothing less than a half tank).
- ➢ Keep up with maintenance on vehicle (spare tires are a must).

Weapons: (gun shop, sporting goods store)

- ➢ At least 9MM handgun or above.
- ➢ A 12 gauge shotgun or rifle .308 or larger.
- ➢ Extra Magazines
- ➢ 500 rounds of each suggested.
- ➢ Ammunition reloader
- ➢ Gun powder
- ➢ Lead (check tire repair shops for lead tire balances).
- ➢ Long bow with arrows and additional bow sting.
- ➢ Hand axe
- ➢ Knifes

Generator: (sears, RV lots, public works, phone company service buildings)

- ➤ 4000 watt generator or higher is suggested.
- ➤ Extra gas may be wise to have stored with the generator.
  - ❖ RV's come with generators normally good enough to power all your appliances in the vehicle. They can run appliances in your home too.

Tools: nothing is worse than getting stuck without the right tool for the job.

- ➤ Hammer
- ➤ Screw driver, hex head and straight headed.
- ➤ Allen wrenches, metric and standard.
- ➤ Wrenches, metric and standard.
- ➤ Pliers
- ➤ Specialty tools for each machine you have in inventory.

Survival gear: Army Navy surplus store, Dicks Sporting Good, Bass Pro Shop, Cabelas and Dunhams.

- ➤ Canteens, Camelbak
- ➤ Flashlight, candle, lantern
- ➤ Knife 6" or longer
- ➤ Knife sharpener
- ➤ Fire starter, matches, lighter
- ➤ Lint: Pockets tend to be great fire starting material.

- ➢ Binoculars (range finder is a nice tool)
- ➢ Compass (GPS may not be reliable)
- ➢ Maps
- ➢ Watch
- ➢ Mirror (signal device)
- ➢ Extreme weather solar blanket
- ➢ Rope or 550 cord
- ➢ Fishing line (100 feet or more)
- ➢ Weapons cleaning kit
- ➢ Ruck sack/ large back pack
- ➢ Survival radio, (these normally can recharge phones by using a crank and other items. They also have them in solar).

Check your packed survival items at least every 3 to 6 months to ensure: expiration dates haven't expired and materials are still intact. When items are stored in a storage unit temperatures begin to take a toll on your items. Plastic sweats when moisture is present, this will cause mold. Also, critters such as spiders and mice like dark moist areas.

Raft/ boat/ and RV/ tent:

- ➢ Picking an inflatable raft is straight forward. Find a durable raft that has the option for a motor.
- ➢ Boats are nice but they are expensive and too large to transport easily.

> ➤ RV's are nice but if their isn't gas you don't go anywhere and with roads not being maintained you would have difficulty moving across terrain also once the LP or Propane runs out their will be no heat.
> ➤ Tents differ in quality. Just think about camping in the winter. Would you want a flimsy tent or would you like one that holds up to wind and snow? Consider getting a tent that can allows for a wood stove.

Survival Tin

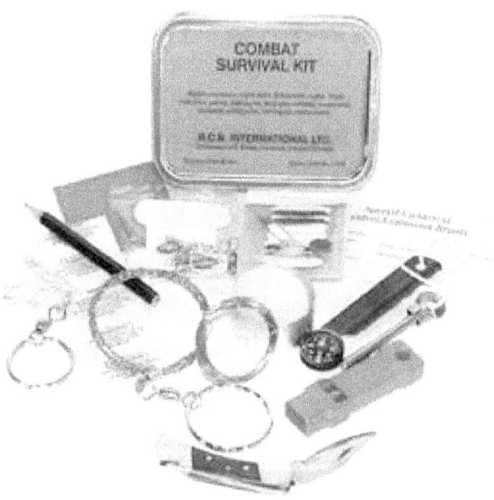

Creating and carrying a survival tin increases your chance of survival and who knows may come in handy one day when you are out and you need start a fire, cut down a tree or just need a pencil to write down something.

Different survival sites and books say different things but it really depends on what you are able to fit in the tin and it depends on your environment. I created my tin off of the diagram SAS Survival guide provided in their book with a few slight modifications based on cost.

Tin packing list:

- ➢ Altoids breathe mint tin can.
  - ❖ Can be used for cooking.
- ➢ Small compass
- ➢ Pencil
- ➢ Mirror or polish the inside of tin.
- ➢ Magnified glass, "As seen on TV" credit card size.
- ➢ 10 water resistant matches, (tape the striker to inside of tin).
- ➢ 4 Chem lights, (ones used for fishing).
- ➢ 5 Band-Aids
- ➢ 2 allergy pills
- ➢ 4 safety pins
- ➢ 4 paper clips
- ➢ 2' snare wire (picture hanging wire)
- ➢ Tea candle
- ➢ 2 cotton balls
- ➢ Fish hook

- ➢ Sinker
- ➢ 20' Fishing line
- ➢ Razor blade
- ➢ Needle with long piece of thread.
- ➢ Wire saw
- ➢ 4 Butterfly bandage
- ➢ Tape (optional)
  - ❖ I used electrical tape to tape the tin shut to keep it water proof, this tape can be reused.

Physical and mental challenges

  A lot of survival books might not mention that you need to be physically and mentally prepared to survive extreme conditions. When it's freezing outside you wouldn't be able to go inside for a warm cup of coffee. If you are hungry you might not be able to go to the fridge for a snack. Preparing for that now will save you from the reality and pain later. Think about it, a kick boxer prepares himself for a fight by practicing for the match. He might spar with someone and take a few blows to the head to be sure that he is physically and mentally prepared for the fight. This is no different in surviving whatever may lie ahead.

  Try starving yourself. See how long you can last without eating. Try two days if the pain isn't too bad go for a third. Caution: don't starve yourself beyond your means. I don't want you to kill yourself or cause damage to your body. Supplementing water for food will help with the pain but remember that you may be limited on water too in extreme situations. In the winter camp out for a night and feel what it's like to live in a tent in extreme conditions.

Body fat, people with a lot of fat may not survive as well as someone who is physically fit. Body fats are good for long periods of famine but try climbing a mountain with a few hundred extra pounds. Start hitting the gym. You will need to be able to bench at least your weight. Get down to less than 20% body fat. If you smoke, "stop now". Your lungs will need to be at their best.

Chapter 2

Get the Gear

Web gear, TA-50, Ammo Vests things only used by militias and the military, right? Wrong. They carry much more than ammo. These also carry water, rain gear, first aid kit, emergency rations or whatever else you think is important to your survival. If for some reason you lose your G.O.O.D. bag or it is stolen then what you have on you has to make do. Many different designs from all over the world are on the surplus market. Plus, designs are made on the civilian market for camping, hunting, mountain climbing, etc... The equipment we will be talking about is the LBE, (Load Bearing Equipment) LBV, (Load Bearing Vest) and MOLLE, (Modular Lightweight Load-carrying Equipment).

Starting with the LBE, the basic pieces are the suspenders, (H or Y-style) and the pistol belt. On the belt you had a combination of ammo pouches, butt-pack, canteen pouches, lensatic compass pouches, (consider having more than one in case one compass breaks) and anything else you could fit on the LBE you think you may need.

Drop bags, (pouches for empty magazines) entrenching tool carriers, flashlight pouches, NVG bags, (Night Vision Goggles) and GPS pouches can be mounted to the LBE.

Typically, a small pouch called a first aid pouch was placed on the suspenders on your non-dominate hand side. Meaning if you are right handed it goes on your left shoulder with the open end facing down, (but closed). Inside the pouch is a military Field Dressing. New compression dressings aka, "Israeli Dressings" do not fit well inside these pouches. The reason it's worn that way is because you typically raise your rifle to your dominate sided shoulder this prevents the butt stock from blocking the dressing. Facing the pouch down makes it easier to pull the dressing out especially if your dominate hand was the injury site.

LBEs are cheap and will work if all you want is a basic system for an emergency kit. The only problem is that it gets heavy on the shoulders after a while.

(lensatic compass pouch)

The next evolution resulted in the LBV. It still uses the pistol belt and pouches but replaced the suspenders with a vest. The vest is adjustable with drawstrings in the sides and straps with buckles on the front. The shoulder pads are wider than the LBE which makes it more comfortable with heavier loads. The front of the vest has 4 pouches: 2x double magazine and 2x single magazine for the M-16. There's a grenadier version of the LBV that replaces the magazine pouches for the M-16 with holders for 40mm grenades. The only issues with the LBV is the vest itself it only holds 6x magazines, (combat load requires 8 magazines) and it doesn't have pouches inside the vest for maps, etc...

Back in the late 90's one company selling a deluxe LBV came with these features but these are not common on the surplus market.

The next step is MOLLE gear. This is a modular system, "the Cadillac of the series". There seems to be an infinite number of pouch designs and patterns for pretty much every weapon or purpose imaginable. These are also capable of mounting MOLLE camelback carriers, IFAK, (Improved First Aid Kit) and many other types of specialty pouches. Some are capable of being attached to pistol belts, (allowing you to use ALICE pouches) some have a MOLLE style pistol belt attached and some don't require the belt because the vest has enough mounting points for all your needs. This system is expensive. There are sets on the market that are supposedly ready to wear with all the pouches. These sets are usually a grab bag that includes pouches you don't need.

If you go with MOLLE get the basic vest and buy the pouches you need for what you carry. MOLLE pouches also work on Interceptor Body Armor and other plate carriers.

These are just three options issued to the U.S. military over the last 20-40 years. As with any piece of equipment first, decide what you are using it for and what your requirements are to meet that purpose. Then decide how much you are willing to spend. With the LBV the MOLLE pouches can be mounted to the belt.

If you plan to carry an M-16, M-4 or AR-15 variant as a survival weapon then the LBV is a better option. If you want a vest only for canteens, first aid and survival kit then the LBE is probably a better option. If you are carrying a rifle other than the AR-15 and have the cash, MOLLE is your best option.

Rucksacks are back packs with metal or plastic back supports built in or on the outside of the pack. They hold much more equipment than your vest can. Medical rucksacks used by the U.S. Army are larger and can carry much more equipment. It has many more pouches for additional equipment. It can get heavy when packed so be cautious on what you pack and where you pack it. Pack heavier items closer to the frame of the rucksack this keeps it closer to your back and wont tip you over backwards.

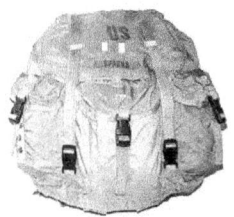

(Standard Military issued Rucksack)

(Civilian hiking backpack)

(MOLLE Rucksack)

Your sleeping bag, clothing, extra ammunition, food, extra water, medical supplies and many other things can be stored in the rucksack. The rucksack provided by the military has a higher weight restriction than a civilian backpack so choose wisely when purchasing yours.

Ghillie suits are used to break up the human form in order to hide you in the wood or in a field. Obviously you wouldn't look right walking around the city or laying in your freshly mowed front yard in one of these but in the wilderness they prove to be worth their weight in gold.

Used by the U.S. Army Snipers and other military special ops teams these suits have allowed our troops to maneuver undetected within enemy lines.

Chapter 3

The Art of Lock Picking

Not every door you come to will be unlocked and not all windows will be accessible if the door is locked. If you don't want to alert anyone of your presents it might be wise of you to learn how to pick locks. MIT created a great manual on how to pick a lock a link will be provided below. Just knowing the basics to picking a lock will be extremely helpful. After locking myself out of my own home 2 times and having to pay a lock smith 50 dollars each time to spend 15 seconds opening my door, I decided to learn how to pick a lock.

Scrubbing a lock is the easiest way of opening a typical house lock. There really isn't much to it other than a little pressure on the pins and rubbing a pick across the key pins. I managed on my first try to open my gun case lock in less than 30 seconds with a simple set of tools.

Scrubbing

1. Insert the S pick and torque wrench. Without applying any torque pull the pick out to get a feel for the stiffness of the locks' springs.
2. Apply light torque with the torque wrench. Insert the S pick without touching the pins. As you pull the pick out apply pressure to the pins. The pressure should be slightly larger than the minimum necessary to overcome the spring force.
3. Gradually increase the torque with each stroke of the pick until the pins begin to set.
4. Keeping the torque fixed, scrub back and forth over the pins that have not set. If additional pins do not set release the torque and start over with the torque found in the last step.
5. Once the majority of the pins have been set increase the torque and scrub the pins with slightly more pressure. This

will set any pins which have set low due to beveled edges etc.

Note: Link to MIT Document.
http://www.lysator.liu.se/mit-guide/MITLockGuide.pdf

(Basic lock picks set)

999 key or a bump key can also be simply made or purchased if you wish. What it basically is, it's a typical house key that has been filed down to the grove (see picture). Only problem is you need to have all the different style of house keys so you can match up the right one for the right lock, so naturally it can add up to a lot of keys. If you decide to make your own Bump Key, be sure to test it on a lock that isn't currently being used to secure something of value to you. If not properly made the key will get stuck in the lock and you will end up having to take the lock apart to retrieve the key.

(999 Key or Bump Key)

Putting the bump key in all the way and pulling it out one pin and adding slight turning pressure (binding) you can tap the key with a screw driver or hammer making the pins jump. When the teeth on the key go past the key pins and all the key pins get stuck they are forced past the sheer line allowing the plug to turn freely. All you are doing is using the manufactured defect of the lock to open it. Simple, quick and effective, but slightly noisy, if you want stealth get the lock pick set. If you want speed get some bump keys.

Knowledge is power

We all know we aren't experts at everything. A mechanic doesn't know how to do surgery and a doctor might not know the first thing about fixing a broken belt on a car but with manuals and technical books we can overcome these obstacles. Mechanical, electrical, electronics, and more need to be on your list of things to have. Dictionary is also a good thing to have considering we all don't know every word in the English language and some technical words are even too technical for me. Even though I have instructed you on survival techniques, it is still important to find further information that might not be in this pocket guide.

Learn how to prepare your own meat if you hunt. You will have to clean it. Considering many may not know how to hunt they won't know how to gut an animal either. Gutting, cleaning and cutting meat is not easy and you can waste a lot of meat and even taint it if you don't do it right. I will talk a little more about preparing game later in this guide.

Learn how to fire a weapon. Take lessons from some of the schools NRA offers and you might learn a thing or two about how different elevations can affect a shot. You can also learn how wind affects a shot and how to figure out how fast the wind is blowing at the target. Ammunition is scarce so think about one shot, one kill. Also with firing a weapon comes maintaining your weapon. If you never took a gun a part start learning today. Know where the dirt hides on a weapon and the best way to clean it. It also wouldn't hurt to know how to take the trigger mechanism apart too. If something was to fail in the trigger not knowing how to fix it might cost you a weapon. If you shoot bow learn how to restring a bow and how to fletch arrows. Practicing a few hours a week shooting targets to build up your accuracy and acclimate yourself to your weapon will help you become more proficient at firing your weapons. Be sure not to break into your stash to practice. Use separate rounds for practicing and have your survival ammunition locked up and ready to go.

If you served in the military you might already know that hand to hand combat is important to know. In battle if you run out of rounds it's time to get up close and personal. Knowing some combat techniques will be important to know. I'm not talking about karate look at a more violent and effective martial art techniques, (I suggest MMA style) and learn as much as you can. Learn pressure points, take down techniques, punching and kicking styles. Weapon combat is also great to know like knife fighting or even staff fighting.

While we are on the subject of the military, techniques of concealment is also important to know. Do you really want to advertise you are camping out alone in the middle of the woods? Knowing what is concealment and what is not, is going to be very helpful. It's also important to know that noise travels far at night and so does light. Keeping sound and light to a minimal level is important to surviving alone. Smells are also more detectible than you may know in the wilderness. Smoking will give away your position in a heartbeat. Study your surroundings or as they say, "when in Rome, do as the Romans do". If the birds chirp all day and for some reason they aren't chirping something might be wrong. A squirrel doesn't build his home in bright colors so think about how you would conceal your camp. Cats bury their business after they are done, (they do this so that nothing can track them).

Learn from your surroundings the animals that live there have been doing this for much longer than you. Reading military manuals like FM 21-76 on Survival or the Ranger hand book will instruct you on concealment and other wilderness survival techniques.

Find books on tracking and which plants are edible. See a foot print on the ground it could be a meal or it might be your worst nightmare. Have a book with a list of tracks or start learning today what different tracks look like. Knowing what plants have healing properties and which are poisonous will save you a lot of grief down the road.

What do you do when you run out of supplies? Well don't wait till the last minute if you see your food supply dwindling to nothing, be prepared to take a trip into a town or city. You might even find small communities popping up along your way that might be willing to trade for things you have. Gas, batteries, ammunition, and other survival things will be very valuable to others. Don't give up much but when you do give it up for a high price. Never travel with all your supplies unless you want it taken from you. Only take what you plan on trading. Scavenging will most likely become a daily activity. Look in places most people won't and you might be surprised what you may find. Not everyone would think of looking at the trash dump but you might find an old generator that may need a simple part to get it running. Most likely stores and malls will be cleaned out of anything worth taking so that is why it's important to look in the more uncommon spots. Industrial places might have tools and most have cafeterias. Great place to score some grub.

   If you happen to find a tent community on the road they most likely will have their own form of security or law. When entering the community you may be asked to give up your weapons. Don't give your weapon to anyone you don't know. Observe from a distance if people are surrendering weapons at the gate, either stash your weapons without being seen or have a friend or relative hold them for you as you go in. Giving up your weapon may cause you some problems. You may not get it back or if you do get it back, it could have been tampered with or your ammunition could be missing.

Who to trust

It's human nature to trust people that's why we are in the current situation we are in today. When we see someone hurt we get a reaction to want to help them. Even the toughest person from the hood has a feeling of wanting to help. Don't be fooled by this. People will hurt you and take what you have.

Police, medical, fire rescue and military, all these people are suppose to be the people we turn to in time of need. That's why people will use this to lure their prey in. A man in uniform has a gun and looks like a police officer but how do you know and what does it really matter after a huge catastrophe. If there is a collapse of the government because of a great disaster, (Do you think that officer still has a job)? Do you think the military will still be acting under the guidance of our government? If the military is still intact they may be enacting martial law. In that case they will take your weapons from you and most likely ship you off to some camp until they have everything under their rule again. Don't think that the military will have your best interests in mind or that they are the answer to everything.

Seeking relief

If seeking medical attention, understand hospitals will be overloaded with patience, low on staff and have very little supplies. Hospitals just aren't equipped to help their entire community at one time. If you have medical supplies of your own bring them along. Keep the supplies secure and on you at all times. We don't need medical personnel treating everyone with your personal supplies. Remember it's in their interest to help everyone they can and if you have additional supplies that could potentially help others they will want it. If for some reason they want to strip you of your stuff, pass it off to a loved one or someone you trust to hold your things.

  Theft can happen anywhere even in a hospital. Bring food and water too just like Katrina, (hurricane disaster) food and water will be rationed and there will be a lot of fighting over what is being rationed. There is also a good chance that if your condition isn't severe you might be turned away. Expect very long delays being seen it's not based on a first come first serve basis in hospitals. People with more severe injuries will be seen first. So depending on your injury you may not be seen at all.

Chapter 4

Staying Home

    Ok so you don't want to leave your property. Well let's think about what we need to keep our home safe. First think about a fence, just like the Alamo you need a big wall to keep people out. So look at getting a good fence, electric is a nice deterrent and guard dogs are always nice. That's if electricity is still available. Get off the grid and you may be able to have electricity after a disaster. Razor wire in front and on top of your fence will slow people down or even deter them from trying all together. Signs that warn people of dogs and guns are a great deterrent to some but could be a great warning for them to be on the lookout when sneaking up on your home.

In the home we need to have a safe room, one with no windows or noticeable entrances. The room shouldn't be noticed as an identifiable room from outside the room or any other room. If I walk into the house I shouldn't know you have a safe room without you telling me. If you have an escape door or tunnel it should lead somewhere that would be hard to find. The room should be as large as you can possibly get without making it noticeable that there's a void in the home. For example, if I walk into your house and in the center of the house is a big wall that I can skirt around without finding a door it will seem odd to me.

It reminds me of a time I was working on a Dish Network installation at a man's house. He wanted Dish in his bed room and in his kitchen. The existing cable he had in the kitchen was not rated for Dish. The line ran into a wall behind the cabinets but when I went around to see where it came out I ran into a closet in the bed room. I went outside and didn't find the cable either, so I asked the man if there was another room he wasn't telling me about. He said, "I was the first to notice" and he showed me the secret door into his safe room, (through the closet) and there was the cable I was looking for. The room was about 12' X 12' and contained his most valuable stuff. He even had a safe in his safe room, (something to think about).

  Safe rooms should contain most of your valuables and items you don't want stolen in case of a break in. You also want to have space for the people who live with you in the shelter until the coast is clear. Having a way to relieve yourself is also a good thing to think about when building this room. The room should be made of reinforced steal and/or concrete. The door should be lockable from the inside. Electricity if any should be ran separately from existing home electrical system and maybe a battery backup system should be in place.

  If you hire someone to build you this room consider hiring someone out of state. Hiring someone local might cause an issue when the contractor starts blabbing all around town about your new room.

Basement rooms are best you can make an escape tunnel from that room or even have a separate room under the floor. The lower floor also muffles sounds better and it's harder to determine if a room is actually a room and not an outer wall. Escape tunnels can lead out to open fields or they could go into an old barn. Just hide the exit. Fake tree trunks make great exhaust vents and no one would be the wiser. If you are heating the rooms don't use heaters that exhaust smoke. Corn/wood burning stoves will end up acting as big smoke signals and we don't want to alert anyone of your presence.

Solar power and wind power are two great options to think about in case of a power failure. Being independent from the electrical grid allows you greater freedom in where you place your home and who will know life exists there. Having a well to get water is perfect and this is why I don't want you living in the city. City water normally will become undrinkable from contaminates after a disaster. Make sure the water you are drinking comes from an underground spring and not a river near your home. Some rivers that flow from a city could be contaminated. Consider creating a water purifier, (instructions will be later on in this guide).

Farming is important to supplement your need for can goods and other processed foods.

If you don't have a green thumb, I am sure you got the book on it like I mentioned before. Also consider learning how to can your own vegetables. Small farm animals like goats and chickens are great sources of food like eggs, fresh milk or meat. Large animals like cows eat too much and may be more costly to take care of than they are worth. Besides we want to be able to hide our animals in case of an emergency. Cows are just asking for someone to come by and kill or steal them.

If you have a diesel vehicle, you can make Bio-fuel to power this vehicle with very little conversion. Search the internet for the instructions and the kit to make the fuel. Bio-fuel only has one drawback; it gets too thick in the winter and can make the vehicle harder to start. For other vehicles that are gas powered you could create a wood-fuel device to attach to the vehicle to power it (plans later in this guide).

Generators are great for power things in a home on a cloudy day. If you don't have access to one but have access to a power washer motor, or a small engine you can make your own. With a few batteries, AC/DC inverter, engine, alternator and a fuel source such as the gasifier you could build one yourself. If you have solar power you may already have enough batteries to power the house and can tie in your motor to that.

Hot water heaters burn up a lot of gas and if you don't have access to LP or propane tank, where will you get hot water from? With hoses on the roof you can make your own hot water much hotter than a hot water heater can produce. I will show you how to make a solar water heater later in this guide.

Now that we know how to make our home run self sufficient you can find a remote location to build this home or one you can purchase and make the modifications as described above. Understand parts will wear out and fail so having spare parts on hand will save you a lot of headaches later. Many things can be purchased already made just search the internet for kits. Also understand that these alternative sources are not 100% going to get you off the grid, unless you make some life style changes. Shorter showers, fewer lights on in the house, turning down the heat and many other changes that conserve energy and water will have to be made.

Picking your location is a very important decision you want to be near a water source but being right next to a lake or river might give up your location. So try to stay within a mile of a large water source. Living near mountainous areas might deter people from coming near your location just for the simple fact they rather go around than over a mountain. Also a mountainous backdrop can block someone's approach. You might want to think about avalanches when building next to a mountain. You take the bad with the good.

Highly wooded areas are great for concealment and finding an abundance of food but can also leave your home vulnerable to forest fires. You also don't want trees too close to your home just for the simple fact that they provide cover for people advancing as they attack. I would rather have a wide open range to see my attackers coming than a forest full of concealment.

Picking high ground is great to protect against floods but being too high up might make your position stick out like a light house on a clear night. Now don't be too concerned about being attacked in the country just consider your chances of being attacked much less in the country than in a town or city.

After a disaster remove road signs and other land marks around your location. This also deters people from venturing down unknown roads. Normally if I can find it on the map (GPS) and its paved I will travel down it to get to my destination. If you have a mail box at the road side, "remove it". Reflective road markers should be removed also. Drive ways should look unused sprinkle grass seed over the drive way so the grass will grow and hide the drive. Find or build your home away from the road have a wooded path that leads back to your property or at least give your home some great distance from the road. If there are no trees consider fencing by the road around your property. Have a second fence with barbwire or razor wire attached to it surrounding that. Look at prisons to get a good idea of what your property should look like. Your entrance should have obstacles blocking the way. Make it so the vehicle approaching will have to travel at a slow rate of speed to maneuver around the obstacles.

Deep trenches along the side of the road will also make it difficult for vehicles to drive around the obstacle course. Bright lighting system should be aimed at on coming vehicles windows. Temporarily blinding the driver gives you the advantage to killing your enemy. Muddy fields also make it hard for foot soldiers to attack. Low level barbwire strung knee high all over the field makes it impossible to run and difficult to crawl under. This tactic has been used by the military for years. Spikes sticking up from the mud also can hurt people trying to advance on your home. Basically if you can't hide your presence make your presence very difficult to get to. Give the aggressor the idea you don't want to be messed with and that you mean business.

Setting up a Shelter

If you are not in a home or a camper you may find the need to make your own shelter. Having the right equipment is always nice but not always necessary to survive in the woods. Utilize what the woods have to offer. Vines and some bark make great rope. Leaves, bark and moss make great roofs and we all know what works for walls. The best way I find to make a hut is to bend smaller trees over and tying up the tops together to form a dome. As long as the roots are still in the ground and the branches haven't broken from bending the trees will continue to grow. Having the root system still intact will also keep your hut upright in extreme weather. Use branches interweaved between the bent trees to form a roof structure. When you are done it should look something similar to a plastic strap lawn chair.

If you have a poncho or tarp you can use this to make a better roof, if not peel bark off fallen old trees the bark should look like shingles. Lay the bark side by side starting at the base of your roof and layer them as you move up close to the top. It should look similar to the roof of a chinese home. You can also use shoots of long field grass or hay. If there is a corn field nearby consider using the stalks. Once you get to the top of the roof use one row of bark and lay it sideways across the peak. All your bark should be half moon shaped as if you had the bark of a split log. Your hay should be laid out tied in small bundles the strands pointing up and down the roof. Use vine to tie down the bark or hay, like strapping down a load on a truck. The vine should secure it and keep it from blowing away.

 For the walls I would figure out where you want the door to be and the windows. Windows are great for circulating the air in the hut and help light the place during the day. Consider placing doors and windows out of the East, because normally winds come from the West.

- ➢ Use sticks tided with vines to form windows before creating the walls. By now you should have at least four bent trees and a few polls tied between them to make windows. Once you have that figured out find the straightest polls and drive them a few inches in the ground forming the wall.
- ➢ Use more vine to interweave between the polls to secure them.
- ➢ Use shorter polls to meet up with the lower part of the window.
- ➢ Use cut polls when you interweave the upper half of the walls loop once

around the small cut polls to close in the upper half of the window.

For the door lay out as many polls, (ones long enough to close off the hole left for door) that you need to make your door fit the opening you left. If the opening is too large consider barn style doors. Now use two boards to lie across the top and bottom of the boards you have laid out and one diagonal almost creating a big Z.

> ➤ Use vine to secure the boards together.
> ➤ Use another board about six inches longer than the door to act as a pivot point.
> ➤ Tie it allowing 3 inch overhang on top and bottom drive the bottom into the dirt giving about ¾ inch clearance to the base of the door.
> ➤ Loosely tie the upper part of the board with vine or rope to the upper support beam.

Try to be as level as possible to keep the door from swinging open all the time. You can use rope or vine to make a loop handle and it can also act as a door lock if you find something to hang the loop over when the door is shut.

This would be a hut where you could tie living trees together. The roof could be large leaves or bark.

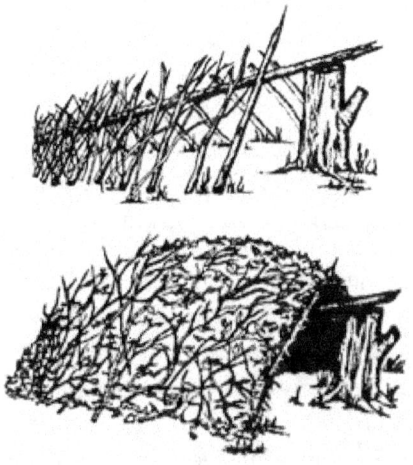

The debris hut is a faster more temporary shelter. Build all your shelters on a sight incline to allow water runoff in case of rain. **Never,** build in a ditch or gully in case of flooding. Use a shovel to create a small trench about an inch to two inches deep around the hut and have it runoff downhill in order to direct water around the hut. You could build your fire a few feet in front of the hut in order to heat it but be careful of building it too close in case of a fire.

 If you are staying in a hut long term consider my first hut. It's more sturdy and it allows you to move around inside. It's not fun changing clothing outside in the cold. Before it gets to late in the season and frost sets in you could make a mud hole and use the mud to patch the walls in order to create a more wind resistant wall. If it's too late in the season just wait until it snows and pack snow on the walls to seal it up. Just be cautious that you don't get snow packed up on the roof. Snow will melt on the roof because of the interior heat causing ice to form and all that ice is too much weight for a hut. You could be crushed under the weight.

 You shouldn't sleep out under the stars like they use to do in the Wild West. Sleeping without a shelter exposes your body to the cold. If anything throw a poncho over your body to keep the dew off you. If you don't believe me put out an umbrella in your back yard over night and in the morning go check the grass under and around the umbrella. The grass under will be dry, (depending on how high the umbrella was from the ground) and the grass around the umbrella will be wet and cold. On colder nights people could get hypothermia from not covering up. Even if you are lying near a fire don't consider lying out under the stars. It only takes a little bit to build a shelter, a lean to or to find a small shade tree. A fire might burn out while you sleep leaving you cold and exposed.

If you decide you want to build a small fire inside your hut make sure that you are ventilated. You can make a chimney out of a whole or two half pieces of bark tied together and one half moon piece set on top to keep water from dripping in. Secure this to the roof and allow it to drop down into the hut. The longer the chimney sticks out above the roof the less likely you will get a down draft from winds blowing up over the roof. That is why you always see chimneys on homes sticking way above the roof.

Dig a hole with a side vent like I show below for better results try and have the hole the wind goes down outside the hut. Just make sure the fire pit is away from the wall. You wouldn't want to have the wall catch on fire with you in the hut. This type of fire pit is great for containing the fire creating a more efficient burn and heating the ground around you.

In case of rain cover the wind inlet hole with a piece of ½ moon bark to keep from getting water in your hole and putting out the fire.

When digging a hole, make sure the ground isn't too dry or too wet. If you pick a spot that has green grass you most likely will have a good location to dig your hole. The spot won't be too wet or too dry. Using a few sticks you can lay them across the sides of the hole, (not over the fire) allowing you to lay a pot for cooking over the fire.

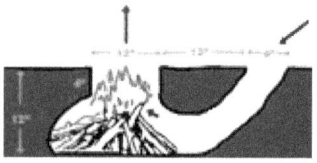

(Dakota Fire pit)

Just because you are living in a hut doesn't mean you should relax on security. Build early warning detection systems. You can do this by using string as trip line or vines and have them holding back a taunt branch that swings out to smack someone in the face. Tying sharpened sticks to the branches will create a lethal trap for your victim. Figure below show a spring spear trap.

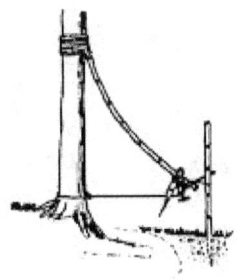

A pig spear trap looks like a bow and arrow setup it is a little more complicated but it makes a great defense system. This setup takes time but can produce better results in capturing food or securing your camp. The spring spear might only wound your intended target but the pig spear trap will most likely kill your target.

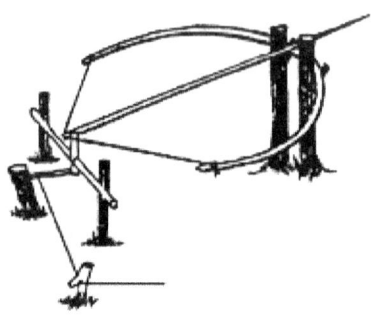

   Understand the wood used in these photos
will dry out and warp into the shape you left
them in and may cause the trap to fail over
time. Regular maintenance of these traps is
required in order to keep them in working
order. If you leave your camping site and move
on destroy your traps so that you don't destroy
an animal and leave the meat to spoil. We also
don't want to harm people that have no
intentions of harming you either. So let's dive
right into security and look at different things
we can do to keep ourselves safe.

Safety and Security

   Whether you are at home or on the move
security is important in your survival. Pull guard
set up regular shifts so that everyone gets a
turn keeping an eye and ear out for trouble. In
the military we pulled guard even on the most
secured buildings or dumbest things like trash.
We had fire guard, staff duty, ammunition
guard, and roving guards. Now obviously you

might not have the number of people to have separate people pulling all these positions. Depending on the number of people staying at your residents you might not be able to pull guard all times. Best thing to do is to try and break the shifts up as much as you can maybe have each person pull two hour shifts.

If it's just two people in your group then you might want to consider pulling dusk and dawn guard. This guard only requires everyone in the group to stand guard when the sun is going down ½ hour after the sun goes down and to be up a ½ hour before sun comes up to pull guard again. Typically, attacks happen around these two times because of the low light situation. It's not as hard attacking in pitch black and it's more concealable to attack in low light vs. during the day. If you are a hunter like myself pulling guard around these two times might provide an opportunity to see some wild game. This goes along with observing your surroundings if you see a deer and it is spooked for no reason this maybe because it senses danger.

Moving down a road, clearing a building, walking through the woods or camping for the night security will still have to be observed. If you are clearing a building someone should always have your back. Never let anyone come up from behind you. If you are compromised in a building and need to flee one man shoots as the next moves down one floor. Then he takes over firing. The next man moves down two floors and takes over firing like leap frog until you are out of the building safely.

  If you are camping in a large group you should set up a perimeter, (if you have enough people to do so) and pair each person up with another person. Have them dig in about a foot deep hole the length of their body, the two holes coming together to form a Y shape. The tale of the Y will be where their equipment hides. One person sleeps as the other lies there pulling guard looking away from the inner circle they have formed. Their feet should be able to touch one another in order to wake the person for their shift or to alert them of danger.

  Let the two people decide what hours they wish to pull for guard. Some like pulling four on, four off, as others like to break it down into two hour shifts. Either way the shifts are hard and staying awake is very difficult. If you need to go to the bathroom let the leader know who is posted in the middle of the circle. The leader and one other person should be taking shifts also staying awake and making sure everyone else who is pulling guard is awake. He/she will typically walk around and relieve people to go use the restroom or to eat chow and stretch.

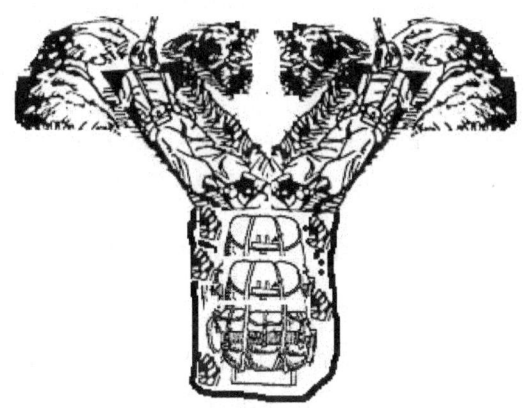

Two man Slit Trench/Fox Hole

Walking in the woods is much harder to do than walking down the road and much noisier too. Typically when walking through the woods you want to be spread out about 50 meters to form a V shape like a duck formation. The front man is the lead man who will navigate everyone through the wood. He has the obligation of making sure the route is clear. He is the one who gives the signals to halt, get down, single file, and move out. The next two should be about 25 meters away and back from the point man, they are responsible for the left and right. The last two are also 25 meters away and back from the middle two, they watch the rear. The leader and second in command will be in the middle of this V. This formation can quickly become a perimeter or a line in no time.

Walking in the woods is hard and slow. You typically run into many obstacles like trees, brush, vines, or even the occasional hill. Its fine to move around these but it's important to keep the V formation as much as possible. The lead man should not get too far ahead and should have eyes on all the men in the formation at all times. It's the leader's job to make sure the point man is notified that he/she is getting too far ahead. At some point you may need to single file the group in order to navigate hard terrain. The reason for the V formation is when you are walking through open fields or in the woods with paths you don't "set your ducks in a row", as some might say. We don't need everyone getting mowed down by an assault rifle. Also walking in a V formation might turn up more items you may need.

Walking along the road each person should be staggered along each side of the road giving yourself five to ten meters between you and the man ahead of you. Lagging too far behind can separate part of the group and running to catch up will not only tire you out it will also hurt the person following you and anyone behind him. So it's very important that you keep up. Following too closely will also endanger you and the man ahead of you. If you walk into an ambush not only is the man ahead of you taking enemy fire, so will you because you where right behind him. If you keep your distance you might be able to maneuver around the ambush and take the enemy by surprise from the side or rear.

If you approach a bridge make sure that each side of the bridge is secured as each two man team passes over the bridge at a time. You don't want everyone crossing the bridge at once just in case someone at the other end trips a detonator and blows up the bridge. You don't want your entire platoon dead. What if there is someone waiting for people to cross the bridge to ambush them? If you are on the bridge you have no place to take cover. So get across the bridge quickly and securely. The lead man should continue to move in order to keep the formation spread out. If you are moving through the woods and come across a road this type of maneuver should be implemented as well.

Chapter 5

Hunting

Unless you are an avid hunter you may not know how to kill and process an animal. Killing the animal is the hard part. Processing an animal is the disgusting part and eating the animal is the tasty fun part we all remember. We are going to have to hunt for it, trap it, or forage for food to eat.

Hunting will prove to be more difficult if you never done it before especially if you don't have the correct tools for the job. Having a gun is so much easier but even bullets run out eventually and that is when you need to start making your own weapons or have alternative reusable weapons on hand. A straight bow, (pictured below) in the long run is a better choice of bow. The string can be removed when not in use preserving the string for a longer life.

Compound bows shoot much faster and go much farther than a straight bow but parts tend to wear out much quicker.

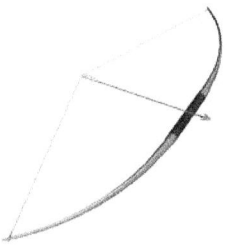

How to make a straight bow

- ➢ Locate an oak sapling that is at least four feet long. Saplings of this length usually have the right thickness to be sturdy and still flexible.
- ➢ Take a sharp knife or other cutting tool and carefully cut away all the branches and bark from the sapling.

- ➤ Whittle the oak sapling into the shape of a bow staff. You won't need to cut anything off the middle of the bow staff but you will need to cut the ends of the staff down to at least a half inch in diameter in order to really give it an authentic look.
- ➤ Carve notches into the ends of your bow. Use your cutting tool or knife to make notches in the shape of the letter "V" into the top and bottom ends of your oak bow.
- ➤ Make a third notch in the middle of the bow staff. Cut a piece of foam, apply some glue to the foam and wrap it tightly around the bow just beneath the notch in the middle of the bow. This will be for your arrow rest and hand grip.
- ➤ Cut a length of Nylon rope that is about six inches longer than your bow. Take one end of the string and tie it to the notch at the top of your bow. Take the other end of the string pull it tight and tie it to the notch at the bottom of your bow. The bow should bend slightly as you tie the string in place.

Heat treating the wood will also make the bow much stronger and less likely to break over time. Heat treating wood is a simple process by holding wood over the fire. The fire chemically alters the wood causing it to bond together making it stronger. In the past hunters would do this to their spear heads after sharpening it into a point.

 If you have the survival tin on you that I describe in this guide you have a snare line that will be great for catching small game.

(Snare trap)

Make a fish hook

 If you forgot your survival tin or lost your last hook in a prize fish you can make a hook. If you have thorn bushes nearby you can make a nice fish hook from the branches. The diagram shows three different possible hook designs but they're actually many other ways to make a hook in a bind. A simple toothpick piece of wood tied in the middle to fishing line can produce results or tying fish bone to a twig to resemble a fish hook also works well. Fish bone is extremely durable and not easy to break.

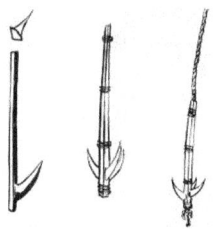

Spears have been used for centuries. A little more difficult to hunt fish with but can produce fish after a little practice. Bamboo is a great resource for making spears but other wooded materials can work just as well. The most important fact in making a fish spear is to have a straight pole and a sharp point on the end that has a hook shape to it. This helps to keep the catch on the spear. A three prong spear works well too, (looks like a pitch fork).

Practice with you spear hitting targets on land first and then try hitting something in the water. If you don't have goggles it will be difficult to shoot under water. Try standing above the water and hitting your target. Understand that objects in water may reflect on the surface and will throw off your aim. Everything may look straight but in reality the object is at an angle. That's why you should practice hitting targets in water before trying to hunt your prey.

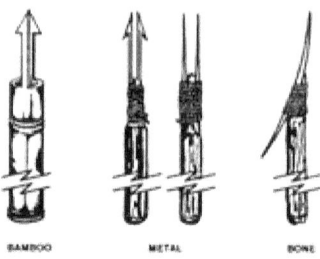

BAMBOO   METAL   BONE

Get the Bait

Flipping a few stones will get you some earthworms or as the saying goes, "the early bird gets the worm". Early in the morning finding worms is much easier than finding them during the day. Worms don't like the heat and will seek shelter underground. A rain storm will drive the worms out of ground because worms can drown. Digging up small plants will expose worms within the root system. You shouldn't have to dig deep to find them.

If you wish to get the bigger fish try using smaller fish. The trick to catching them is either with a screen or fine net. Lay it in the water and wait till the minnows swim over the net, then pull the net out by the four corners. Also stunning fish with a large stone in shallow water works well. If minnows are near shore in shallow water throw a large rock in with a lot of force. This causes a shock wave in the water that will stun the fish for a few seconds.

Gutting and preparing your animal

Gutting a deer is pretty easy but you don't want to rush it. If you cut into the stomach or the intestines you will most likely taint the meat or at least have a nasty smell from it. Some people will do it differently, like hang the animal first and let it bleed out. I prefer to gut the animal right where I dropped it. It saves on having to drag it and string it up.

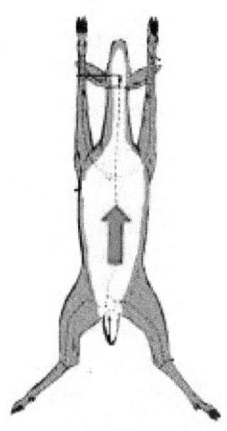

> Pinch the skin typically around the stomach area and pull it away from the stomach. Use a pocket knife to make a small incision enough to get your two fingers in.

- ➢ Use two fingers to push down the stomach and hold the knife between the fingers with the blade pointed up. The pointed part of the knife should not protrude past your fingers. We don't want to risk cutting the stomach.
- ➢ Cut the skin all the way up to the neck. If you're having trouble getting to the neck, use the serrated edge of the blade to cut through the rib cage.
- ➢ Once you get close to the neck cut the throat pulling it down and out of the body.
- ➢ To remove the lungs you will need to cut them away from the ribs. There is a flap of skin holding them to the ribs.
- ➢ Everything else will come out with ease until you get to the anus.
- ➢ To remove the anus cut around the anus trying not to cut too deep. If you cut too deep you risk cutting the intestines and tainting the meat. If done right the anus will come out without spilling its contents.

> ➢ Keep the heart, liver and lungs these things are edible. Tongue, eyeballs and meat on the face are also edible and are pretty good too. Eyes can be eaten raw and are a great source of water.

Skinning the deer

> ➢ With the deer hung by the hind legs make a cut around the legs in a ring manner.
> ➢ Do the same thing to the forelegs.
> ➢ Cut down the rear legs to the crotch.
> ➢ On the forelegs cut down to the leg pits and to the chest.
> ➢ Roll the skin so that the fur roles into itself.
> ➢ Start with the rear legs and roll down.
> ➢ Once to the tail cut around it.
> ➢ Use your fingers to separate the skin from the back.
> ➢ Once you are to the neck the closest point to the head, twist the head in a jerking motion to break its neck.
> ➢ Cut the remaining tissue to remove the head along with the skin you peeled off.

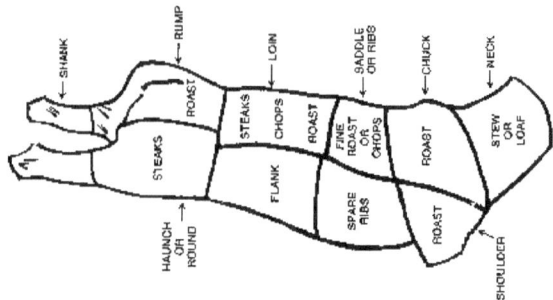

Use the guide above to cut the meat. Don't forget the parts I mentioned above that aren't shown on the diagram. We don't want to waste any part of the deer.

Skinning small game

Small game is different from skinning a deer. You can skin a squirrel with the guts still on the animal. Here you want to make a small incision like we did with the deer. Looking at the diagram we can see that the skin can be peeled away quick and simple. Once it's peeled, you can use your knife to open up the inside in order to expose the guts, (use finger to rip out the guts).

Preparing Poultry

- ➢ Bleed the bird
    - ❖ Hang bird by the feet.
    - ❖ Stretch neck and cut throat.
    - ❖ Allow blood to drain out.
- ➢ Plucking
    - ❖ Dip bird in extremely hot water for a second to loosen up feathers.
        - ▪ Don't do this for waterfowl.

- ➢ Drawing (remove innards)
    - ❖ Make cut from vent to tail and remove innards.
    - ❖ Retain heart and kidneys.
- ➢ Boil bird to insure viruses are killed.

Preparing Fish

- ➢ Descaling the fish
    - ❖ Use a spoon or butter knife and run it against the scales to remove.
    - ❖ Use cold water to rinse fish.
- ➢ Use sharp flexible knife to cut fish.
    - ❖ Get the blade up underneath gill and cut into fish behind head half way.
    - ❖ Repeat on other side of fish.
    - ❖ Cut along ventral of fish to the anal cavity making small cuts.
    - ❖ Once to the rib cage cut along cage to top of fish.

- ❖ Turn knife and run down towards tail.
- ❖ Remove meat
- ❖ Repeat on other side.
- ➢ Discard of bones and guts.

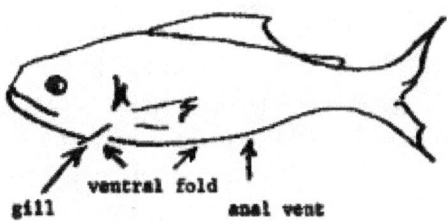

gill   ventral fold   anal vent

Preparing Pork

- ➢ With pork you don't want to skin it you should gut it. Place it over hot embers of the fire.
- ➢ Use hotter than normal water to help scrape of the hair.
- ➢ Set out water and paper towels for clean up after dressing is done. If you are wearing a long-sleeved jacket or shirt, remove it to avoid making a mess.
- ➢ Take your knife and make a circular cut around the hogs' anus. Cut deep into the pelvis until the anus is free.
- ➢ If the hog is a male cut off the penis and testicles and sever the urethra close to the anus.
- ➢ If a female, include the genitals when plugging the anus. This area should pull

through the pelvic opening when the intestines are removed.

- ➢ Make a small slit in the abdominal wall, being careful not to cut the intestines. Work slowly pulling the intestinal wall up and cutting with the knife blade facing up. Slit the abdominal wall from the bottom of the ribcage to the pelvis.
- ➢ If the hog is small split the ribcage by cutting off to the side of the sternum. Split the ribcage and continue the cut as far up the neck as possible.
- ➢ If the hog is large it may be difficult to split the ribcage. If that is the case continue the cut over the ribcage by just cutting the skin.
- ➢ When past the ribcage continue cutting deep next to the windpipe as high as possible up the neck.
- ➢ Sever the windpipe of a large hog as high up as possible and then cut around the windpipe where it enters the upper chest this is similar to cutting the anus.
- ➢ The windpipe should pull through when organs are removed.
- ➢ Repeat above procedure for the small hog.
- ➢ Cut the diaphragm so the internal organs can be removed.
- ➢ Reach up into the chest cavity and grab the windpipe and chest organs and pull them out of the chest cavity.

- ➢ Cut any connective tissue that prevents the organs from coming out.
- ➢ The diaphragm may need to be cut again to allow the organs to be completely removed.
- ➢ Continue pulling until all chest organs and intestines are removed.
- ➢ Work slowly and try not to puncture the intestines or bladder. The gut pile should include everything from the windpipe to the anus.
- ➢ Turn the hog's chest down to let the blood drain. When finished, use water and paper towels to clean off the blood.
- ➢ Boil to kill parasites and viruses.

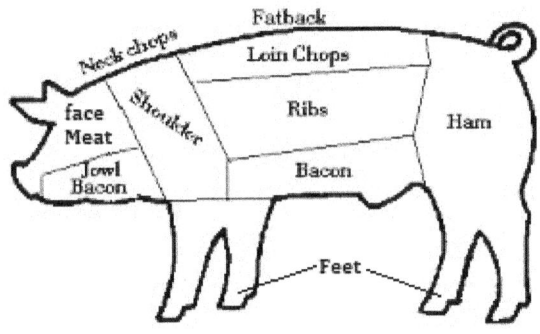

Smoking Meat

  To build a quick smoke house you can use two ponchos snapped together and three polls set up over a fire pit in a Teepee fashion. Smoke pit should be buried into the ground and I suggest using a Dakota fire pit, (shown in Setting up a shelter) in order to keep the fire burning under the poncho. The fire doesn't have to be large, the main thing we want is smoke. Smoke is the key ingredient to a Teepee smoker. Don't use pallets or any other materials that have chemicals in them. Use hardwood because hardwood is best for producing smoke.

Time line

> ➢ 12 hours of smoke will preserve meat for about 1 week.
> ➢ 48 hours of smoke will preserve meat for up to 4 weeks.
> ➢ Smoke meat will resemble brittle sticks if done right.

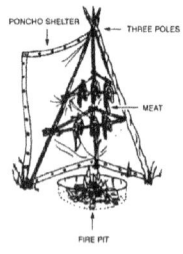

Teepee Smoker

Other means of preserving meat would be freezing meat, (if you live in a cold climate) salt, or drying meat. You could also dig a root cellar, these cellars if dug correctly can keep food cold and fresh for weeks. Digging it too shallow and you will end up with spoiled food. Dig your cellar at least six feet deep if not deeper. Have a pipe come out from the ceiling for ventilation. Heat rises so having a vent only keeps it cooler in the cellar. Some people build these into the north facing side of a hill, (the coolest side in the summer) allowing for walk-in access. A simple one could be dug in like a man hole and have ladder access.

Wrap food in something to keep bugs out. Dig a ditch in the cellar to channel rain water. Stay away from large trees when digging, (roots from the tree may cause difficulty when digging). Clay is a great insulator packing it on the roof of the cellar will keep heat out from the mid-day sun.

Chapter 6

Knowing your senses and what that does for security

Security is really being aware of your surroundings. Knowing what lies ahead and what is behind you is only the basics to security but is very essential. Using all your senses: hear, sight, smell, touch and taste are all key to staying secure. With hearing listen to what is around you use your hands and cup them around both ears in order to make a funnel effect. Sit quietly for a few minutes and just listen. Remember all the sound you hear and try to write them down. Do this in different places where you travel to get a sense to what you should normally hear. Understand sound amplifies in the winter after a good snow fall. Sound is more likely to be absorbed by leaves and grass. Doing these exercises will strengthen your listening ability and will heighten your awareness. Also it's pretty relaxing to do this in the woods.

  For sight we first should have corrected vision of 20/20. I don't suggest wearing contacts in the field dirty hands can cause pink eye and that is the last thing you need in the field if left untreated. Glasses can end up scratched, broken or even lost. Replacing glasses will be much more difficult after a disaster. If you plan on wearing glasses consider the ones that change shades in different light. This saves you from having to carry two sets of glasses or a pair of clip-on.

  Did you ever wonder why pirates wear an eye patch? No it's not because they are missing an eye. It's so that they can see in the dark. Have you ever walked into a dark room and had to take a minute to adjust to the low light, (Pirates would lift the patch once in a dark room and they could see fine, giving them the advantage when they fought down below in the gully of the ship). I am not saying you should go around wearing an eye patch but in situations where you frequently need to transition from day to night, I would consider it. The only down fall is depth perception greatly reduces when one eye is covered and the fact that you can't see from one side is also another down fall.

When you think of sight you think being able to see, well also look at sight as being able to detect things. Use flash cards of different silhouettes of known objects to train your eyes to identify shapes. This sends a signal to your brain that registers an object. Being able to identify them quickly will help in surviving in an extreme combat situation. I also find those picture games in the bar, (you know two photos and you have to find the differences) to be fun and a great way of practicing your skills. If you are not color blind, (unlike me) you should also train your brain to detect colors. A wrong shade of green can stick out like a sore thumb if your eye can catch it and your brain can register it.

Smells are very important to understand. Is that wood smoke smell a forest fire or a wood stove? Deer use the sense of smell to detect when danger is near. That's why hunters don't run to the woods after splashing on cologne.

Smokers you will find your sense of taste and smell are greatly desensitize over everyone else's because the body becomes use to only smelling one thing and it also lingers on your clothing and on your breath. With humans our weakest sense is smell we don't know when our own breath stinks or if it's been one too many days for a shower. We need to be aware of this and think about what smells are around us. When hunting try and stay down wind of your objective this way you are not detected.

Feel, everyone might think they have this one down pat but how many truly can feel the slightest touch? In California where earthquakes are a regular thing tremors go unnoticed by the locals there. The reason why is they lost their sense of feel to that sensitivity. It's common to feel tremors so your brain doesn't register the feeling. Many people, where I live in Michigan didn't feel the earthquake tremor that hit recently. It was less than a rumble when a car goes over a bridge it goes unnoticed by the general public. How about getting bit by a mosquito? Do you even feel them land on you most the time? Heighten sensitivity to feelings like this can help. Knowing when the temperature drops a degree may be signs of something happening in the atmosphere, like a cold front. Understand the weatherman may not be there to tell you what's coming. Preparing for a cold front may take longer in the field vs. if you where at home. It's no different when it's going to rain. You feel a drop hit you and then it gradually increases. Do you wait till it's a down poor before you take shelter or do you move out of the weather before it hits? It's the sense of feeling that helps us out when other senses fail.

Now consider feeling when you have no other sense to help you. It's dark so your sight is useless there are no odors to smell, no sounds to guide you and all you can rely on is touch. How do you tell what you are touching? Well in the home you may know by common things you have in your home that you are use to but how about in the wilderness. You touch something wet or something jagged. Do we dart our hands out to grab the object or do we slowly and gently feel its shape? Well many, like a child would try and grip it and pull it towards them to investigate their new found toy. You don't want to do that in a dangerous environment. Using one sense requires you to use your brain more to gather information and process it. Your brain will work harder in order to come up with an answer. That is only because it normally relies on all the other senses to come up with an answer. Look at blind people, they can read brail by just one sense, (sense of touch). If they can train their brain to read brail or to tap a stick to figure out where they are going, so can you.

Try an exercise where you walk around your home or in your back yard blindfolded and see if you can figure out where things are at. Train your brain to think quickly to signals coming from your touch. Your brain will want to remember movements, like did you turn left and how many steps you took.

In a hostage situation you are tied up, gagged and throw into the back of a dark van. You can't see where you are going and can't hear anything over the loud radio or thick insulated walls. So you rely on your sense of touch! Immediately start counting, (20 second took a left) and feel for shift in weight, (130 seconds hit a bump and braked on second bump). Look for bumps that might indicate railroad tracks. If you know where you started from and you know generally which direction the van left in you can get a general idea from what you are feeling and where you are going. If it took only 20 seconds to make a left it must mean they turned on the first block and you know by now that three streets down are a double set of tracks that are in need of repair. So as you can see focusing your brain to think about what information is coming in just from one sense can help you determine your surroundings and may save your life.

Also in a kidnapping it's important that you control your emotions and focus. Listen to their voices, (try to listen for names and possible places).

Taste is a sense that is just as important as the rest and like the other senses it can determine a lot of things. For instance, in checking plants and fruits to see if they are edible you need to taste. If you taste a burning sensation on the tip of your tongue it may be a sign that it is poisonous.

Chiefs are great at this sense. They can combine the spices of the world and create something that will make you melt in your seat. They do this by training their sense of taste, (along with smell) combining them into a wonderful combination. Now many people don't taste when they eat they cram it in their mouths and chew a few times allowing it access to our throat and down to our stomachs, (not giving it time to sit on our tongue allowing us to fully engage in its glory). Slowly savoring food can give us indication if something is tainted in our food before we digest it, giving us time to spit it out.

Staying knowledgeable gives you a sense of control. Knowing ahead of time where you are going or what is coming will help you stay calm and will give you more time to react appropriately. Using your senses greatest abilities will help you achieve this. Practicing each sense individually will help your brain distinguish between the signals its getting and will help in the response from the brain.

Hand-to-hand combat

Let's be truthful not all of us are born fighters. Fighting doesn't come naturally to all people. Some have less pain tolerance than others but the fact remains one time or another in our life we will need to know how to fight. In hand-to-hand combat you have to come to terms that you are most likely going to get hurt. The only question is will you hurt your opponent even worse?

MMA, (Mixed Martial Arts) is one of the leading styles of fighting today and now is being adopted by the U.S. Army. It's normally a combination of Brazilian Jiu-Jitsu and kick boxing. Though these two fighting styles are not the only fighting styles in MMA, it is one of the leading techniques learned today.

Never underestimate your opponent. It doesn't matter what they look like they might know more than you do and brute force may not be enough to win the fight. If you dislike being punched you should either become a great runner or learn how to take a punch. In MMA you learn defense as well as offence. You will start in many different positions in training to learn how to defend yourself. Training is intense and brutal. I can't tell you how many bruises, bloody noses and pulled muscles I came home with but like tattoos even though they hurt its addicting. As training goes on I became better. Learning on how to land a submission move was the highlight of my training. There's no better reward than submitting your instructor for the first time.

Submission moves

Arm Bar: wrapping your legs around a person's arm and you drive your pelvis into his elbow while pulling back on his wrist hyper extends the person's arm. This is a very painful move if done correctly and can cause serious lasting damage to your opponent.

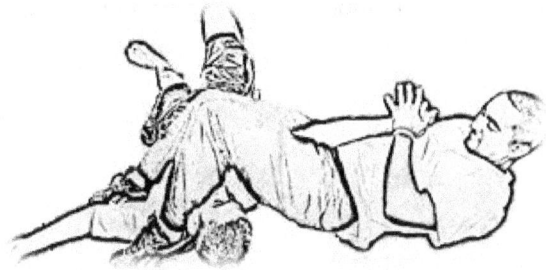

Leg Bar: Just like the arm bar only difference is you have a person's leg wrapped up as you drive your pelvis into their knee cap.

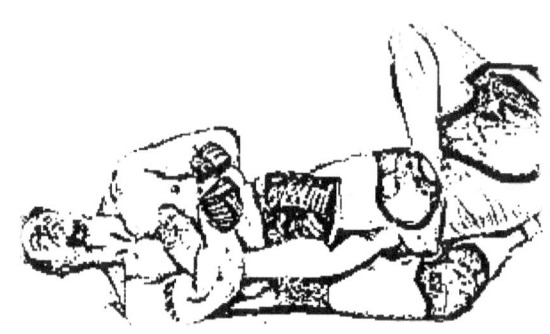

Kimura: Taking the person's wrist on the opposite side the body you are on and rapping your arm up under their arm and grabbing your own wrist then pulling the arm back like you are twisting his arm off. In the picture below, this can be done in either direction from above the head, (back behind the opponent) or from the waist, (back behind the opponent). It just really depends on which way his arm is laying when you pull this move.

Triangle Choke: a chokehold which strangles the opponent by encompassing the opponent's neck and one arm, your legs wrapped in a configuration comparable to the shape of a triangle.

Ground & Pound: a ground fighting tactic consisting of obtaining a top dominant position and then striking the opponent with fists and elbows.

Punching:

Punching isn't as simple as making a fist and throwing a hook. A lot of science goes into a punch. You have to watch for an opening, balance, pin point your target, shift weight, punch, block and much more. To throw a good punch you first have to have a good balanced stance. The dominate hand you put all your power into, should be to the rear and the same sided foot needs to be back a half step from the other foot, (shoulder width apart).

The other hand is your jab hand and that should be in front. Your body needs to be erect but not so much that it puts you off balance. Knees bent slightly, the heal of the rear foot slightly off the ground. Your elbows need to be into your chest and your hands by your head to block any shots to the head. Your chin on the forward shoulder and the body twisted at the waist like a twisted rubber band ready to unravel.

This stance is uncomfortable but being in the ready is important if you want to get a shot in that will count. Now we can look at a jab, using the non-dominate hand jab it out like the, "Rockem Sockem Robot" but don't over extend and don't leave it hanging out there. Get it back into the ready and follow it up with a power punch, (the old one—two).

Aim for the eyes remembering this is only a jab not a power knockout punch. It's only designed to stun the opponent, (allow for you to fire off the second punch). Never over extend your shot we don't need to be set off balance or leave yourself open for a knockout. It's ok to miss the shot just having your hand out there to block there view is a good enough opportunity to get in a power shot. When hitting with a jab make sure that the majority of your body weight is shifted forward onto the side of the body you are throwing the jab on. This is how you keep your balance when striking. While your jab is coming back into the ready it's time to unwind at the waist and shift your weight to the other side by turning your heal of the rear foot outward.

The head should always be looking forward at the target the shoulder touching the chin. Allowing your waist to give you the force you need to punch, not just the arm. At this point your jab hand now becomes the rear hand and should be a great setup for a hook.

When trying for a hook you don't want to flail your arm around like you are a pitcher. Allow your shoulder and waist to do the swinging and turn your arm into an L shape. Don't over extend this shot. Once your shoulder hits the chin your swing needs to return to the start position. Don't forget weight distribution and keep the opposite hand at the ready to block a return shot.

The more you practice these techniques the better you will become at fighting. Understand this manual will not make you an expert at fighting so seek further instructions by a professional licensed instructor.

Chapter 7

Fallout Procedures

After a disaster happens you should have about an hour before fallout occurs depending on the location and the type of disaster. Volcanic eruptions, as long as you are not right next to the volcano I am sure you will have a few hours if not days before the ash starts to hit the ground. This is the time you should be seeking long term shelter. Your vehicle needs to be equipped with at least a half tank of gas. Have all your emergency items ready to go, (grab it and move out). Make sure road maps and GPS have the coordinates and alternate routes laid out before hand. Allow a few extra hours for road hazards, traffic backups and other situations.

If you are caught in the fallout while moving:

- ➢ Stop the vehicle, leave the vehicle locked and windows rolled up.
- ➢ Put on protective gear and gas mask if one is available.
- ➢ Use a cloth to cover mouth and nose if nothing else is available.

- ➤ Do not run the AC unless you have it set to recycle the air inside the cab, (Understand the air filter may become clogged with thick ash from a volcano).
- ➤ Consider running a hose from the air filter into the cab through the firewall in order for the air filter to obtain clean air.

If you are on foot seek shelter immediately. If no shelter is available use a poncho to cover up while you get on protective gear. Try moving under shelters and trees to avoid direct exposure. Subways, sewers, and other underground accesses will provide slow but safer passage throughout the city. If you are in a sewer follow the flow of water it should lead you out of the city to an open water source or to a waste management complex depending on what sewer system you are in.

Seek vehicles that most likely are unoccupied. City bus garages or school bus garages should be helpful when looking for a free vehicle that is topped off and not locked, (just push the center of door to open). Worst thing you may have to do is break into a building or jump a fence to gain access to these vehicles. Don't bother with car lots most cars there usually are filled with less than a ¼ tank of gas, (to prevent thievery). Breaking into a locked car and hotwiring it is much more difficult than taking a school bus.

Keys to the buses are normally in the bus garage locked up in a thin metal box that can be opened with a pry bar and the keys are labeled for each bus.

Stay protected at all times even while you are temporarily under shelter. Nuclear fallout is very dangerous to your health long term exposure to this is not pretty. Ash from fires or volcanic eruption can burn the lungs, causing major health problems and toxic poisoning from the fumes. If you need a gas mask or protective suit look for the closest fire station they have all this equipment on hand including oxygen. The fire truck will also have first aid and other essential survival needs on it including a full tank of gas. This might be a good mode of transportation.

Those within 25 miles of a nuclear explosion who are not protected will likely receive a lethal amount of radiation which can be deadly after a few hours of exposure. Within 80 miles exposure to nuclear explosion can cause death within two weeks of contact that has not been treated. After 150 miles contact to fallout can cause severe internal damage with a loss of white blood cells causing your immune system to weaken making it easier for you to get sick. Those who are 250 miles away from a nuclear blast will experience a loss of white blood cells but will not experience immediate symptoms.

Cleaning yourself after radiation exposure is extremely difficult because the particles are like fine sand that sticks very well to objects. Soap and water won't be enough to clean off the contamination.

After exposure

After being exposed to the blast wash thoroughly with soap and water primarily the exposed skin and hair. Do not scrub your skin as this might rub in the radioactive sand. Before entering your shelter remove your clothing but do not brush off the dust. Brushing off the dust will cause the dust to become airborne and may enter the body through the nose or mouth, (causing more exposure issues).

Chapter 8

Staying Hydrated

Staying hydrated is important and I know at times finding water will be hard to do. It's important that you stay hydrated especially in windy conditions. Eating snow is not recommended you get little water out of snow and the coldness of the snow can reduce your core temperature causing you to freeze to death. If you do need to use snow melt it first and consider heating it. Melt a little at first, add more as it melts to avoid making air gaps that will evaporate the water underneath and leave snow on top. Here are some tips on how to find water.

If you are in the forest cutting fresh vines can give you clean water on the go. Know what vines to cut first. If the vine comes out clear and not milky then you are in the clear. Don't expect much but every drop counts.

If you are resting overnight you can use plastic to collect dew, have it funnel into a bottle or a hole in the ground. Moisture collecting on the plastic throughout the night drips down into the cup giving you drinking water in the morning.

Rain can be a good source too but I suggest boiling it first depending on the environmental disaster. Pollutants after a disaster can make the water almost undrinkable. Water purification tablets are an alternate solution to filtering your water. They help take out bacteria's that are found in water. Look for fast moving streams to find the purest drinking water. In the desert water can be found under the ground or in cactus plants. Chewing different plants can extract water but be sure you aren't chewing something that is toxic.

Another way of hydrating is by enema. If the water is too dirty to drink going through the anus is much easier and it hydrates you much more efficiently. Camelbacks would be a good way of administering yourself the water if you can't find an enema kit.

➤ Take the tip off the camelback and insert the tube into your anus, (Making sure it's secured and won't come out).
➤ Lying on your back with the camelback elevated is the best way to allow the water to flow in.
➤ Once the water is gone from the camelback remove the tube and try not going to the bathroom for at least 30 minutes, (This gives the water time to be absorbed into the system).

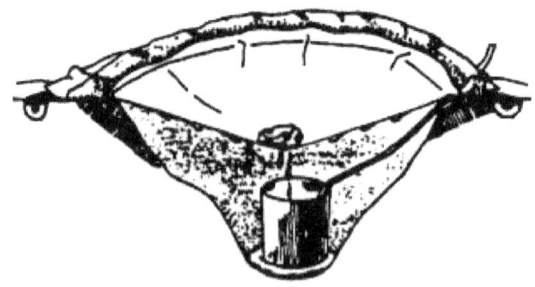

The picture above is a solar still. As you can see it's a cup in a hole with a piece of plastic covering the hole with a rock weighing down the plastic sheet. When water is poured into the hole, (not in the cup) the sun over the course of the day will make the water evaporate and the evaporation is caught on the plastic. The rock is used to weigh down the plastic so the evaporation that collects on the bottom of the plastic will roll down and drip into the cup. A drinking straw allows you to drink from the cup without having to lift the plastic tarp. Pack dirt around the edges of the tarp to close off any gaps that would allow air to escape. Gaps allow evaporation to escape making you lose much of your drinkable water.

Fruits and plants

How can you tell if a fruit is toxic or not? Cut it open and smell it if it smells like a peach or almond it's poisonous. Avoid any weed, leaves or seeds with an almond like scent, (an attribute of a cyanide compound). Test it on your skin if you get a rash it's not safe. Next, test it on the lips if you feel a burning sensation it's not safe. Then chew it a little and spit it out. If you don't feel sick within an hour try eating a little piece. Wait another hour if you don't get sick it is safe to eat. This is why its better having books handy on plants than trying to test everything. You may not want to have to wait a few hours before being able to eat.

Before testing a plant for edibility, be sure there are enough plants to make the testing worth your time and effort. Do not waste time testing a plant that is not plentiful in the area. Eating large portions of plant food on an empty stomach may cause diarrhea, nausea or cramps so eat in moderation.

Plants can be tested in the same manner. First separate the parts of the plant into roots, stem, leaves and make sure no part of the plant has worms or other plant eating insect on it. This is a good indication that it could be rotten. Don't eat plants or fruits that have been on the ground. Pick it from the source in which it came to be safe.

To avoid potentially toxic plants stay away from any wild or unidentified plants that have:

- ➤ Milky or discolored sap.
- ➤ Three-leaved growth pattern.
- ➤ Beans, bulbs, or seeds inside pods.
- ➤ Bitter or soapy taste.
- ➤ Spines, fine hairs, or thorns.
- ➤ Dill, carrot, parsnip, or parsley like foliage.
- ➤ Almond odor.

➤ Grain heads with pink, purplish, or black spurs.

Things you can eat commonly found in North America.

Pine Tea, which can cure scurvy and is a great source of Vitamin C takes minutes to make and will help warm the body on cold nights.

➤ Grab a handful of pine needles about 1/4 cup is all you need (fresh only).
➤ Place in boiling water for ten to fifteen minutes.
➤ Add lemon and/or honey if available.
➤ You now have 100% of the US RDA requirement for vitamin C.

Dandelion flowers are plentiful in most of North America and many don't know they are edible and good in a salad. The younger the flower the more sweet it tastes. Leaves from the flower are good steamed. Day lilies are another type of common flower that you can eat. Hibiscus petals are also sweet tasting or can be dried and used for making tea. Dry the leaves in the sun and use pantyhose to make a pouch similar to a tea bag and dip it into hot water for a few minutes depending on the strength of tea you prefer.

Mushrooms are easy to find in Michigan and other forests throughout Northern America and are most easily found in the early spring. There are 12 species of mushrooms that are deadly and there is currently no cure for mushroom poisoning. Make sure you know the mushroom is edible and when in doubt don't eat it. As far as my guide to testing poisonous plants I wouldn't suggest testing it on mushrooms. Just knowing which are edible would be the safest bet.

Morels are one of the easiest wild mushrooms to correctly identify and is one of the most sought after wild mushrooms. Morels are hollow with a pointed wrinkled cap. Morels should not be eaten raw. They grow wild in woodlands near dead and dying hardwood trees such as: elm, birch and maple.

The chanterelle is another wild mushroom that is editable. Chanterelles are an orange color with a trumpet-shaped cap. Chanterelles can be found growing in moderate woodlands in late summer and early fall.

Honey mushrooms are known locally in Michigan as "stumpers". They are major parasites of rotting trees and tree stumps where clusters of them are found growing in the northern hemisphere world-wide. It is named, "honey" because the color of its cap looks like the color of honey. Their round caps flatten out at maturity. Honey mushrooms are toxic when raw and must be cooked thoroughly before eating. There are several poisonous mushroom varieties with similar appearance and therefore shouldn't be sought after unless you can properly identify the mushroom. Honey mushrooms have white spores while their poisonous brothers have brownish spores.

Insects

Venomous Spiders:

- ➢ The black widow spider is identified by a red hourglass on its abdomen.
- ➢ Brown recluse spider is a small light brown spider identified by a dark brown violin on its back.

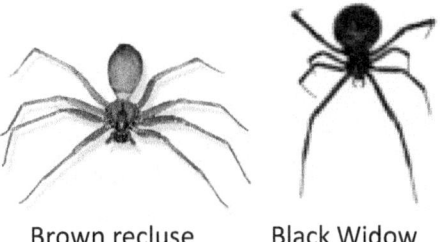

Brown recluse   Black Widow

Other harmful insects:

> ➢ Fire ants (painful stings cause swelling and allergic reactions have caused death).
> ➢ Bees (reported cases of killer bees in North America).
> ➢ Scorpions (though scary only 25 know species can actually kill humans out of 1752 species).
> ➢ Centipedes (known to kill infants, stings can cause severe pain and swelling).
> ➢ Mosquitoes (Not venomous but can transfer diseases).
> ➢ Flies (not venomous but can carry diseases; maggots are good for cleaning out infected wounds).
> ➢ Ticks (not venomous but can cause disease).

Chapter 9

Medications

Certain tree barks are known for their properties of reducing fever, pain and inflammation. A special ingredient contained in these barks is one of the most powerful pain killers in nature.

Fever, muscle aches, osteoarthritis, headache, menstrual cramps, arthritis and inflammations including: bursitis, tendonitis and traumas such as: a sprain can all be treated with a dose of natural salicin made from the bark of these trees. Salicin concentrates in the inner bark of trees and shrubs related to willows which include:

> - Populus Tremuloides: Quaking, Trembling or American Aspen, (Northern & Western North America).
> - Populus Grandidentata: Bigtooth Aspen (Eastern North America, South of P. Tremuloides)
> - White Willow/European Willow (Salix Alba)
> - Black Willow/Pussy Willow (Salix Nigra)
> - Crack Willow (Salix Fragilis)
> - Purple Willow (Salix Purpurea)
> - Weeping Willow (Salix Babylonica)

Simply cut into the bark and strip it off. Since the interface between the bark of the tree and its woody portion is very slippery you can peel the bark off in long unbroken strips. Either, chew the strips of bark as long as you don't mind the bitter taste, (fastest results) or boil it in water to make a tea. Consider adding pine needles to delude the taste.

Creating your own soap

Wood ashes have been used for centuries as a source of lye in the soap making process. When lye is mixed with fats or oils a chemical action takes place that produces soap. Do not use wood ashes to wash your body or any gear that cannot withstand harsh soaps. Ashes from hardwood trees are better for making soap.

To clean dishes select the largest pot you want to clean. If the food residue is not very greasy you can help the soap making process by adding a small amount of fat or oil into the pot. Butter, margarine, olive oil, animal fat, etc... are all good to use. Just a few drops are enough. Add a few cups of ashes into the pot. If there are bits of charcoal mixed in with the wood ash that is even better since charcoal will aid in scouring. Add enough hot water to the wood ashes in the pot to make a paste.

The hot water will create potassium salts from the wood ashes which will then mix with the fats or oils in the food residue. This forms a crude soap that will cut through the crud and grease on your cooking gear. When the water and wood ash paste is cool enough smear it all over your cooking gear and let it set for several minutes. This is where the chemical reaction takes place that makes your wood ash soap.

First Aid

In an extreme survival situation you don't want to use your medical supplies to treat other people. The reason you may need it later, if you used it you will end up a stinky creek without a paddle. Also understand you take a risk treating others such as: HIV or TB. Look at the situation, is the person old? Is there immediate danger to your own life? Is treating this person worth the risk, (meaning is he/she going to die anyways, no matter if you treat them)? Not trying to sound impersonal or disconnected but really you have to consider if this is a lost cause. Treating the wounded person first starts with checking him\her completely over from head to toe.

Please note that before you look over the victim you will want to protect yourself. Wash hands before putting on clean gloves and roll up sleeves. Consider putting on a mask to keep from getting sick, (the person may be suffering from an illness and you don't need to be catching anything they might have).

Things to check for:

- ➤ Is the victim conscious?
- ➤ If conscious ask them what the injury is?
- ➤ If not conscious check for a pulse and breathing.

- ➤ If no breathing but has a pulse check the airway and begin CPR, (see CPR section).
- ➤ If victim loses pulse while you are treating he /she do CPR, (see CPR section).
- ➤ If victim has no pulse and is not breathing do not treat, (Don't know how long person has been expired).
- ➤ Check for bleeding, (see bleeding section).
    - ❖ Start from the head and work your way down to the toes.
    - ❖ Do not attempt to move victim unless dangerous conditions warrant a move.
- ➤ Check for broken bones. Apply pressure dressing if bleeding but not over broken bones.
- ➤ Check to see if person is in shock, (see treatment for shock section).
- ➤ If no pulse and no breathing victim may have been dead for some time don't do recovery.

Burns

Burns destroy skin which skin regulates the amount of heat our bodies retains, hold in fluids and protects us from infection. While burns on fingers and hands are usually not dangerous, burns injuring even relatively small areas of skin can develop serious complications.

- ➢ Treating a burn begins with stopping the burning process.
- ➢ Cool the burned area with cool running water for several minutes.
- ➢ Look for blistering, sloughing or charred (blackened) skin.
- ➢ Mild burns with reddened skin and no blisters may be treated with a topical burn ointment or spray to reduce pain.
- ➢ Cool water, (not cold or warm) may also help with pain.
- ➢ Over the counter pain relievers like Ibuprofen or Acetaminophen can be used for the pain of a mild burn, (typically redness only).
- ➢ **DO NOT APPLY BUTTER OR OIL TO ANY BURN!**

Bleeding

- ➢ Regardless how severe, all bleeding can be controlled. If left uncontrolled bleeding may lead to shock or even death.
- ➢ The first step in controlling a bleeding wound is to plug the hole.
- ➢ Blood needs to clot in order to start the healing process to stop the bleeding. Just like ice won't form on a moving

river, blood will not coagulate when it's flowing.

➤ Put pressure directly on the wound. If you have some type of gauze, "USE IT". Gauze pads hold the blood on the wound and help the components of the blood to stick together promoting clotting.

➤ If you don't have gauze, terrycloth towels work just as well. If the gauze or towel soaks through with blood, add another layer, "DO NOT Replace".

➤ Never take off the gauze. Peeling blood soaked gauze off a wound removes vital clotting agents and encourages bleeding to resume, (only replace if dirt is present).

Applying a tourniquet

 A tourniquet is a constricting band placed around an arm or leg to control bleeding. A soldier whose arm or leg that has been completely amputated may not be bleeding when first discovered but a tourniquet should be applied anyways. This absence of bleeding is due to the body's normal defenses, (contraction of blood vessels) as a result of the amputation. After a period of time bleeding will start as the blood vessels relax. Bleeding from a major artery of the thigh, lower leg or arm and bleeding from multiple arteries, (which occurs in a traumatic amputation) may prove to be beyond control by manual pressure. If the pressure dressing under firm hand pressure becomes soaked with blood and the wound continues to bleed, "Apply a Tourniquet".

The victim should be continually monitored for worsening development of condition. Some conditions may require the performance of necessary basic life-saving measures such as: clearing the airway, performing mouth-to-mouth resuscitation, preventing shock and/or bleeding control. All open, (penetrating) wounds should be checked for a point of entry and exit and treated accordingly.

The tourniquet should not be used unless a pressure dressing has failed to stop the bleeding or an arm or leg has been cut off. On occasion tourniquets have injured blood vessels and nerves. If left in place too long a tourniquet can cause loss of an arm or leg. Once applied it must stay in place. **DO NOT** loosen or release a tourniquet after it has been applied and the bleeding has stopped, (seek medical help).

Improvising a Tourniquet

> ➤ In the absence of a specially designed tourniquet, a tourniquet may be made from a strong, pliable material such as: gauze or muslin bandages, clothing or

kerchiefs. An improvised tourniquet is used with a rigid stick-like object. To minimize skin damage ensure that the improvised tourniquet is "at least two inches wide".

Notes:

> ➤ The tourniquet must be easily identified or easily seen.
> ➤ **DO NOT** use wire or shoestring for a tourniquet band.
> ➤ A tourniquet is only used on arm(s) or leg(s) where there is danger of loss of person's life.

Placing the Improvised Tourniquet

> ➤ Place the tourniquet around the limb between the wound and the body trunk, (between the wound and the heart). Place the tourniquet two to four inches from the edge of the wound site. Never place it directly over a wound, fracture or directly on a joint, "wrist, elbow or knee". For wounds just below a joint place the tourniquet just above and as close to the joint as possible.
> ➤ The tourniquet should have padding underneath. If possible place the tourniquet over the smoothed sleeve or trouser leg to prevent the skin from

being pinched or twisted. If the tourniquet is long enough wrap it around the limb several times, keep the material as flat as possible.

➤ Damaging the skin may deprive the surgeon of skin required to cover an amputation. Protection of the skin also reduces pain.

Applying the Tourniquet

➤ Tie a half-knot, (A half-knot is the same as the first part of tying a shoe lace).

➤ Place a stick or similar rigid object on top of the half-knot.

➤ Tie a full knot over the stick.

➤ Twist the stick until the tourniquet is tight around the limb until the bleeding has stopped. In the case of amputation dark oozing blood may continue for a short time. This is the blood trapped in the area between the wound and tourniquet.

➤ Fasten the tourniquet to the limb by looping the free ends of the tourniquet over the ends of the stick. Then bring the ends around the limb to prevent the stick from loosening. Tie them together under the limb.

➤ Other methods of securing the stick may be used as long as the stick does not unwind and no further injury results.

> If possible save and transport any severed, (amputated) limbs or body parts with, (but out of sight of) the victim. Place amputated limbs in ice if possible.

> **"DO NOT"**, cover the tourniquet. You should leave it in full view. If the limb is missing, (total amputation) apply a dressing to the stump.

> Check and treat for shock.

CAUTION: DO NOT LOOSEN OR RELEASE THE TOURNIQUET ONCE IT HAS BEEN APPLIED BECAUSE IT COULD ENHANCE THE PROBABILITY OF SHOCK.

Treat Shock

Causes and Effects:

Shock may be caused by severe or minor trauma to the body. It usually is the result of:

> Significant loss of blood.
> Heart failure
> Dehydration
> Severe and painful blows to the body.
> Severe burns of the body.
> Severe wound infections.

> ➤ Severe allergic reactions to drugs, foods, insect stings and snakebites.

Shock stuns and weakens the body. When the normal blood flow in the body is upset death can result. Early identification and proper treatment may save the person's life.

Signs/Symptoms

Examine the victim to see if he/she has any of the following signs/symptoms:

> ➤ Sweaty but cool skin (clammy skin).
> ➤ Paleness of skin.
> ➤ Restlessness or nervousness.
> ➤ Thirst
> ➤ Loss of blood, (bleeding).
> ➤ Confusion (or loss of awareness).
> ➤ Faster than normal breathing rate.
> ➤ Blotchy or bluish skin, (especially around the mouth and lips).
> ➤ Nausea and/or vomiting.

Treatment/Prevention

In the field the procedures to treat shock are identical to the procedures that would be performed *to* prevent shock. When treating a victim assume that shock is present or will occur shortly. By waiting until actual signs/symptoms of shock are noticeable, the rescuer may jeopardize the victim's life. Position the victim "**DO NOT**", move the victim or his/her limbs if suspected fractures have not been splinted. Move the victim to cover, (if cover is available and the situation permits). Lay the victim on his/her back.

NOTE: A victim in shock after suffering a heart attack, chest wound or breathing difficulty may breathe easier in a sitting position. If this is the case allow him/her to sit upright but monitor carefully in case his condition worsens.

  Elevate the victim's feet higher than the level of his heart. Use a stable object, (a box, field pack or rolled up clothing) so that his feet will not slip off.

WARNING: Do not elevate legs if the victim has an un-splinted broken leg, head injury or abdominal injury.

WARNING: Check victim for leg fracture(s), splint if necessary before elevating his feet. For a victim with an abdominal wound place knees in an upright, (flexed) position.
Loosen clothing at the neck, waist and wherever it might be binding.

CAUTION: Do not loosen or remove protective clothing in a chemical environment.

Prevent chilling or overheating

  The key is to maintain body temperature. In cold weather place a blanket or other like item over victim to keep the person warm and under him/her to prevent chilling. However, if a tourniquet has been applied leave it exposed, "if possible". In hot weather place the victim in the shade and avoid excessive covering. Try and keep the victim calm. This can be done by being authoritative, (taking charge) and by showing self-confidence. Assure the victim that you are there to help him/her.

Food and/or Drink

  During the treatment or prevention of shock "**DO NOT**", give the victim any food or drink. If you must leave the victim and he/she is unconscious turn their head to the side to prevent the victim from choking, should they vomit.

CPR

1. Check the victim for unresponsiveness. If there is no response call for help and return to the victim. In most locations

the emergency dispatcher can assist you with CPR instructions.

2. Tilt the head back and listen for breathing. If not breathing normal pinch nose and cover the mouth with yours and blow until you see the chest rise, (give two breaths). Each breath should take one second.

3. If the victim is still not breathing normal, coughing or moving, begin chest compressions. Push down on the chest, (1½ to 2 inches) 30 times right between the nipples. Pump at the rate of 100 times per/minute, faster than once per second.

Continue CPR until help arrives or until you are unable to perform CPR anymore.

Fractures

There are two types of fractures: open and closed. With an open, (compound fracture) the bone protrudes through the skin and not only do you have an open wound you have a broken limb. After setting the fracture treat the wound as any other open wound, (Apply a Pressure Dressing). A closed fracture would have no open wounds. Follow the guidelines for immobilization, set and splint the fracture. The signs of a fracture are pain, tenderness, discoloration, swelling deformity, loss of function and grating.

- ➢ Get two branches at least two inches in diameter make sure they go at least six to ten inches past the fracture.
- ➢ Tie the polls above and below the fracture making sure you don't cover the fracture.
- ➢ If you have open wounds treat it with gauze adding to it but not removing.
- ➢ **Don't treat an open fracture with a tourniquet unless you can't stop the bleeding.** You risk creating pressure on the already fractured bone and it may cause more damage.
- ➢ Only apply tourniquet if you plan on not saving that limb. If possible attempt to save the limb.

Sprains

The signs and symptoms of a sprain are pain, swelling, tenderness and discoloration, (black and blue color). A lot of medical journalists will tell you to think the term RICE.

- ➢ R – Rest the injury.
- ➢ I – Ice the injury for 24 hours then heat after that.
- ➢ C – Compression rap the injury or apply a splint.
- ➢ E – Elevate the injured area if possible.

Chapter 10

Land Navigation

Land navigation consists of three basic tools: a compass, map and protractor. Even though it's possible to navigate without these tools it's much more difficult. In the past our ancestors navigated by the stars. Most people these days can't even figure out which star is the north star. Even the art of navigation with a compass is a dying tradition. Replaced by modern technology the compass is second to GPS. What are we to do once the satellites stop working or your GPS unit runs out of battery power? It never hurts to know a different way of doing things.

Lensatic compass

The Lensatic Compass is the preferred compass of the U.S. Army. It's very accurate if used properly. Each part of the lensatic compass is just as important as the next. It's very important that you take care of the compass. Review the picture below to get an idea what everything is. In the military it was common practice to tie a dummy cord to the compass and tie it off to your LBE that way you don't accidentally lose it in the wilderness. When using this compass it is important that you don't hold it near any metal objects. Metal objects interfere with the compass needle and will give you wrong reading. It's also important that you hold the compass level when reading the compass. An unlevel surface will cause the needle to rub on the base of the compass and that too can cause a wrong reading.

The cover lifts up and has a sight line or dot that can be used to pin point objects ahead this can be used as a reference point when walking. Combined with the rear sight slot, you get a more accurate reading. The rear sight also has a lens that helps you see the azimuth on the compass. The short luminous line turns like a knob and can be set to north for a quick reference guide. Just open the compass up point north to the line and you are now on course. When the compass is not in use, push down the rear sighting slot to lock the compass in place. This prevents damage to the compass.

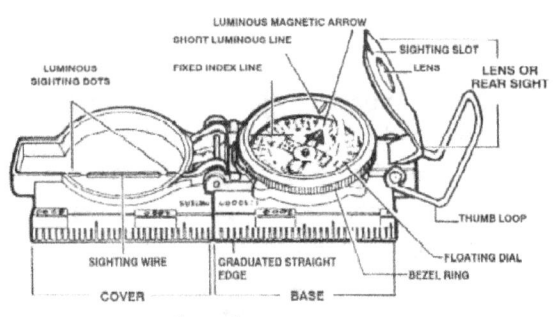

Lensatic compass

Map Reading

A Grid Map has grids that represent one kilometer or as we say in the military one Klick, (Yes, it's spelled correctly). These grids are almost like the lines on a civilian map when you are trying to locate a road and it says 1A. If someone gave you coordinates to a bunker you would do the same as you would on that civilian map.

Why is it important to know the difference between <u>Grid North</u> and <u>Magnetic North</u>? If you look at the picture below you can see a few degrees of difference. These degrees vary depending on where you are at in the world. When getting your azimuth from a map using a protractor you have to either add or subtract a few degrees to compensate for magnetic north.

If you don't do this and you march a few kilometers you might find yourself far off course. The reason is the Grid North and Magnetic North are two different locations. Many may think that the North Pole is where Magnetic North lies and when they open their compass up they expect to be pointing towards the North Pole. This is not the case because Magnetic North moves constantly and currently is located somewhere over Northern Canada and heading to Russia at a rate of 40 miles per year. Instead of constantly creating new maps to move grids they figured it would be easier to just have you add a few degrees or subtract as needed. This doesn't mean maps last forever. Land shifts, roads are created and Mother Nature does her thing and that is why land surveys are done all the time.

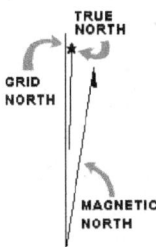

➢ **Grid North**: the direction of a grid line which is parallel to the central meridian on the National Grid.

> ➤ **True North**: the direction of a meridian of longitude which converges on the North Pole.
> ➤ **Magnetic North**: the direction indicated by a magnetic compass. Magnetic North moves slowly with a variable rate and currently is west of Grid North.

Protractor

Protractors are used to figure out the azimuth of where you are going on a map. The outer markings on the protractor show the degrees as represented on a compass. The triangles inside the protractor are for three different scale size maps and are used to figure out how many meters your location is within a grid.

To figure out your azimuth you place the center of the protractor on your current location on the map and use a ruler to line up your destination with the degrees on the outer part of the protractor. If you have a pencil you could draw a line from point A to point B and drop the protractor over the line to figure out the degrees. Then all you have to do is add or subtract Magnetic North and you are ready to move.

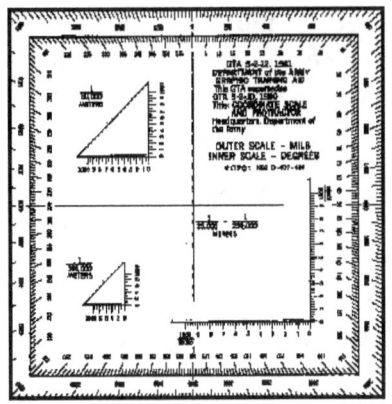

Scales:
1:25,000 x 1km/1:250,000 x 10km
1:50,000 x 1km
1:100,000 x 1km

To figure out your grid coordinates on a grid map you need to have a grid map, a protractor and a known point of position. I say known point because if you are lost and you happen to come upon a map you may have trouble figuring out where you are at.

To figure out your known point of position you could use surrounding land features to get an idea of where you are at. For instance an intersection near railroad tracks or a bridge; might stand out more than a flat open field. If you see an object on a map and it's in the distance you could use the compass to get a heading and use the reverse heading to back track to your location. Again don't forget to compensate for Magnetic North. You may have to judge distance to get a somewhat correct location.

  Now that you have a known location you can get your grid coordinates. Place the protractor on the map making sure the protractor is flipped correctly and is in upright position. Always begin your reading by the southwest corner of the grid.

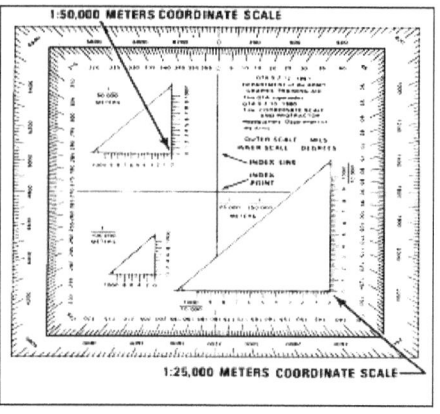

  The number of the vertical grid line on the left side of the grid square is the first and second numbers of the coordinates. The number of the horizontal grid line on the bottom side of the grid square is the fourth and fifth numbers of the coordinates. To determine the third and sixth digits of the coordinates place the coordinate scale on the bottom horizontal grid line of the grid square containing the known point.

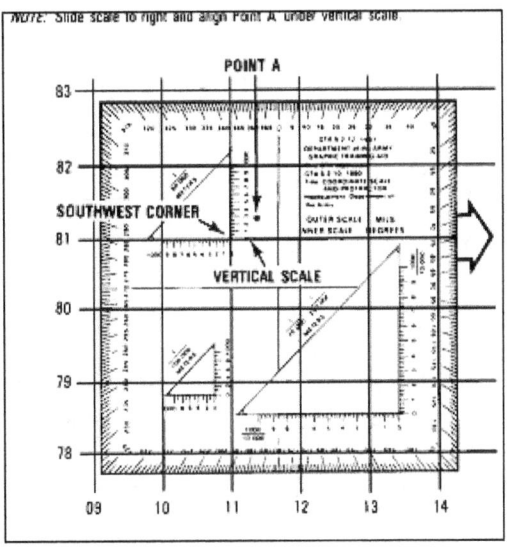

Check to see that the zeros of the coordinate scale are in the lower left-hand corner of the map grid square. Slide the scale to the right keeping the bottom of the scale on the bottom grid line until the known point is under the vertical scale. On the bottom scale the 100 meter mark nearest the vertical grid line provides the third number. On the vertical scale the 100 meter mark nearest the known point provides the sixth number.

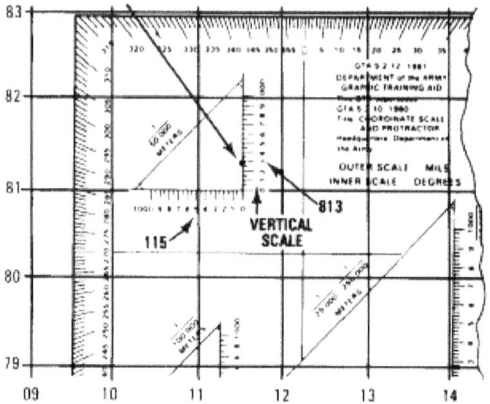

These numbers are important just in case someone needs to locate you. You could relay a message over a radio and give them the coordinates and they could physically map out your location.

Finding north by the stars

Finding North by using the stars is not as difficult as many believe. If you have a clear night sky and you see the dippers, you can figure out where the North Star is. If you can find the Little Dipper you can locate the North Star by looking for the last star that makes the end of the Dipper. If you are unable to identify the Little Dipper, locate the Big Dipper and the two stars that make up the front of the dipper. That acts as a reference point to the North Star as seen in this diagram.

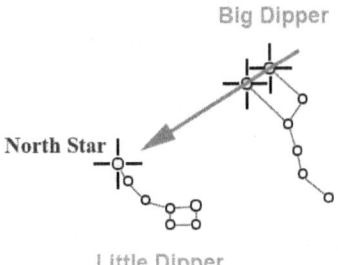

During the day figuring out north it can be simple if you have a watch on. Place the hour hand at the sun, then point between the hour hand and 12 which is south. To figure out north, "just turn around". This can also be done with anything as long as you know what time it is and you can imagine a watch and the hour hand location on a watch.

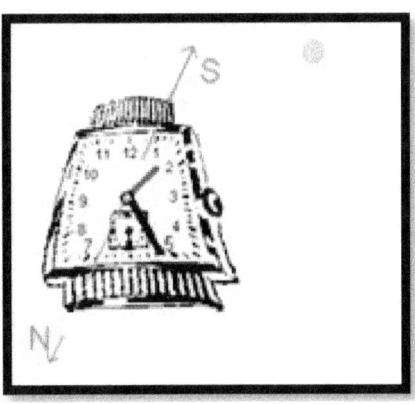

Also for you city people in the Northern Hemisphere if you can't figure out which way is north, look on top of houses or in back yards. Satellite dishes all point south west in the U.S.A. Another way is finding moss on a tree which typically grows on the north side of a tree.

Mark a shadow of a stick and wait 30 minutes then mark the new location of the shadow. This will tell you which way east and west is. If the shadow is getting larger its getting later in the evening meaning the shadow is heading east. If it's early in the morning the shadow will be heading west. Just remember the sun comes up in the east and sets in the west.

Chapter 11

Building Instructions

Wood Fuel Gasifier

What you need

- ➤ Wood Chips
- ➤ Sealed Container to hold the wood chips.
- ➤ Separate fire surrounding the contained wood chips.
- ➤ Hose from the container holding the wood chips.
- ➤ Container to cool gas, (radiator will work).
- ➤ Possible regulator to regulate how much gas goes into carburetor.

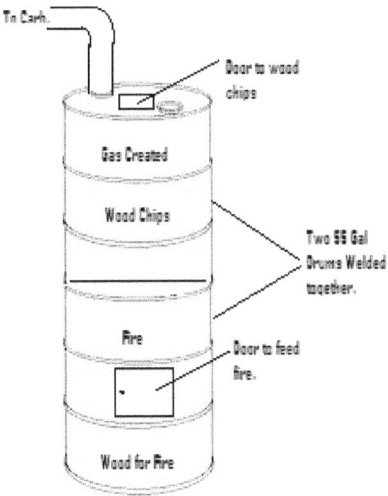

Note:

- ➢ Wood fuel is a gas not a liquid and can be pumped directly into the carburetor.
- ➢ Fire must heat wood chips to 450 degrees in order to create gas.
- ➢ May take 30 minutes or more to create the gas.
- ➢ Vent the bottom barrel to allow air flow to the fire. You can do this by putting hole around the bottom barrel.

Homemade Generator

What you need

- 12 volt car/ boat batteries
- AC/DC Inverter 3500 watts or better suggested.
- Small motor
- Alternator
- Car Battery cables
- Electrical cabling, same used in homes.
- Fuse box (optional)

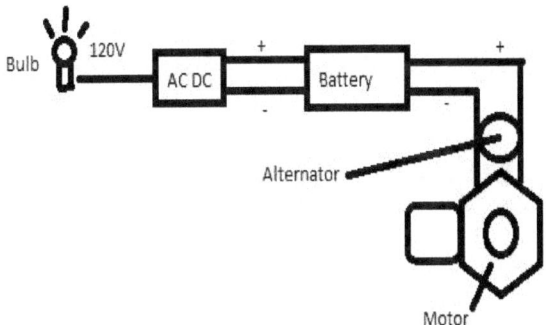

Note:

➢ The more batteries you have attached, the more power you can stored.

➢ Police cars have larger alternators in them. Consider this when wanting to charge a great amount of batteries at one time.

➢ Interconnect batteries in a chain positive to positive and negative to negative.

➢ Do not place batteries on cement floors this will drain the battery.

➢ If batteries are bad try using distilled water in the battery by removing the caps and filling them up to the line.

Water Filter

What you need

- ➤ 55 gallon drum, (plastic is best).
- ➤ Charcoal
- ➤ Sand
- ➤ Clean container to catch clean water.
- ➤ Stand to hold drum above ground.
- ➤ Small holes in bottom of container to release the water.
- ➤ Screening to place in bottom of drum.

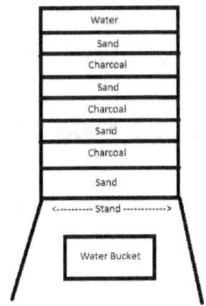

Note:

- ➤ Dirty water goes into the drum, filtering down through the sand and the coal cleaning the water. It comes out the bottom as clean water into the bucket.

Solar Water Heater

What you need

- ➢ Black hose, (rated for 450 degrees or PVC piping painted black).
- ➢ Metal box painted black large enough to house the house setup.
- ➢ Plexiglas to cover top of box.
- ➢ Water source
- ➢ Water storage

Note:

- ➢ Run the PVC or Hose in the box the way a radiator would look from left to right in an S shape.
- ➢ Make sure it's all painted black except the Plexiglas.
- ➢ If it's a rubber hose you can clamp it or glue it to the box. Make sure you seal the PVC piping with proper glue and primer.
- ➢ In the attic place a large container that can contain the hot water. Consider putting the hot water heater in the attic.
- ➢ Run the cold water up to the roof and into the solar panel.
- ➢ Send the hot water line down into the hot water heater or containment device, from there run a line to your hot

water line that distributes water throughout the house.

➤ To keep the water hot throughout the day, consider adding a pump to send the water back up to the solar panel.

➤ There are kits available for this and they are tax deductible to home owners.

➤ www.energystar.gov

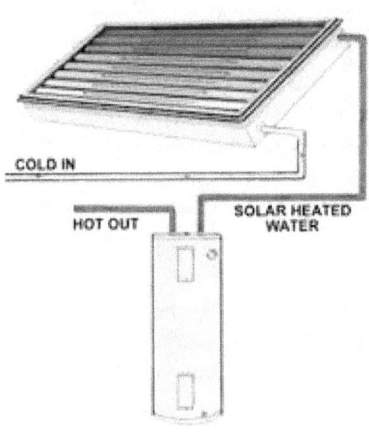

Fire Maker

What you need

- ➤ Two sticks
- ➤ A piece of soft wood.
- ➤ A rock that is palm shaped or a piece of hard wood that can fit into your hand.
- ➤ Shoe string

Note:

- ➤ The picture says it all but let me add if you want to speed up the fire process use some dry lint from your pocket to act as a fire starter.
- ➤ Put lint in hole and rub stick in hole to create smoke.
- ➤ Once it starts to smoke blow on the smoke to create a flame.
- ➤ Make sure the hole has vent through bottom to let in air.

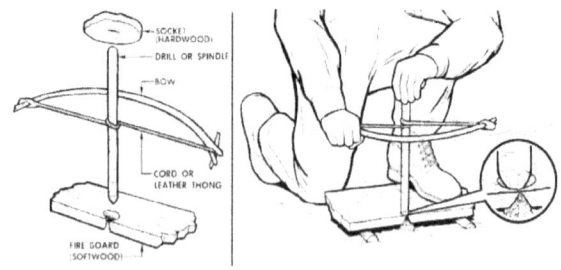

Solar Cooker

What you need

- ➢ Satellite Dish, (Just about 60% of every house in the USA has a dish on the roof).
- ➢ Tin Foil
- ➢ Sunny day
- ➢ Pot
- ➢ Stand

Note:

- ➢ Line the dish with tin foil with the shiniest part up.
- ➢ Use arm on dish to make a mount for pot.
- ➢ Point dish directly at sun.
- ➢ Solar rays can cook food up to 400 degrees.
- ➢ Dish doesn't have to be on a tripod, "you can set it on the ground".

Wind Turbine

What you need

➢ DC Motor, (typically out of a treadmill or hi powered vacuum cleaner).

➢ 8" diameter of PVC pipe, (4' or longer).

➢ Metal tubing for poll and tail fin support.

➢ Hub off of an alternator.

➢ Caster wheel off of an office chair, (pivot point for turbine to turn).

➢ Use sheet metal for tail fin.

➢ Washers, nuts, and bolts.

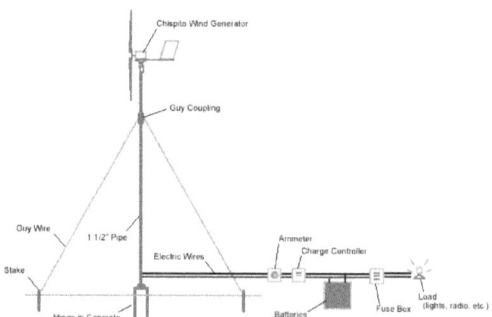

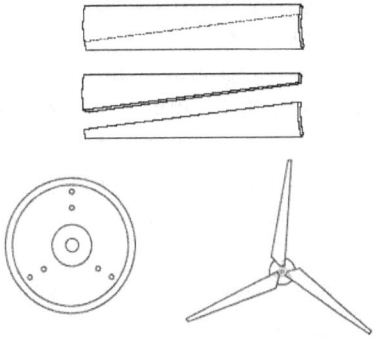

Hub and Blades

Follow the diagram in order to wire it up to your home. **Warning**: this produces electricity, (take the proper precautions when hooking this up).

<u>Char Cloth</u>

What you need

- ➤ 100% cotton cut into small squares.
- ➤ Tin can (Altoids can works best)
- ➤ Create a small fire.
- ➤ Put a tinny hole no more than one centimeter in top of can in order to allow gasses to escape.
- ➤ Place the cut cotton cloth in the tin can gently. Do not drop in can or pack can full of cloth.

- ➢ Now place it on the fire making sure that it will not fall over.
- ➢ It will start to smoke or might even catch fire. Let it burn out and once the smoke stops coming out of hole, remove the tin from the fire.
  - ❖ Do not open the can until it has cooled down.
  - ❖ If opened too soon you risk causing a fire or burning yourself.
  - ❖ Char cloth is used for starting fires.
  - ❖ It is highly flammable and great with the smallest sparks.

Links and References

> - www.extremesurvival.net
> - www.ready.gov
> - www.december212012.org
> - www.survivaltopics.com
> - www.survivalistboards.com
> - www.lysator.liu.se/mit-guide/MITLockGuide.pdf
> - www.greenterrafirma.com
> - www.survivaltopics.com
> - www.insectidentification.org
> - www.equipped.com

Books

> - US Army Survival Manual: FM 21-76
> - SAS Survival Handbook, Revised Edition: For any climate in any situation.

Credits

I would like to thank Brandy Johnson who helped me review and edit this guide. I also give thanks to the U.S. Army Infantry for giving me the seven years of experience.

I hope you have gained some knowledge from this guide and that you use it refer to it often and pass it on to others. Visit **www.ExtremeSurvival.com** to find out about additional publications and join our cause.

Glossary

Authoritative - Able to be trusted as being accurate or true; reliable: "clear, authoritative information".

Azimuth - The horizontal angle or direction of a compass bearing.

Binding - Causing hindrance; restrictive.

Bivy - A temporary encampment with few facilities, as used by soldiers, mountaineers, etc.

Bump key - A lock picking technique for opening a pin tumbler lock using a specially-crafted key.

Camelbak - A brand of water canteen worn as a backpack.

Coagulate - Change to a solid or semisolid state.

Concealment - Any object, vegetation, terrain feature, or phenomenon (i.e., night, smoke, fog) that prevents a combatant (or unit of combatants) from being seen by the enemy.

Cover - Anything which is capable of physically protecting an individual from enemy fire.

Cyanide - Sodium or potassium cyanide used as a poison or in the extraction of gold and silver.

Edibility - The property of being fit to eat.

Encompassing - Surround and have or hold within.

Enema - A procedure in which liquid or gas is injected into the rectum, typically to expel its contents but also to introduce drugs or permit.

Fletch - Each of the feathered vanes of an arrow.

Foliage - Plant leaves, collectively.

Gasifier - A heating device which burns so hot that the fuel turns from a solid state to a gaseous state.

Get down - A command given to soldiers directing them to lie down on the ground.

Grating - Sounding harsh and unpleasant.

Grenadier - A soldier armed with grenades or a grenade launcher.

Halt - A command give to soldiers in order to get them to stop moving.

Klick - A word used to describe a kilometer.

Move out - A command given to soldiers in order to get them to walk.

Muslin Bandage - A very thin cotton cloth used to cover wounds.

Perimeter - The continuous line forming the boundary of a closed geometric shape.

Point man - A soldier who resides at the head of a patrol.

Protractor - An instrument for measuring angles, typically in the form of a flat semicircle marked with degrees along the curved edge.

Single file - A command given to soldiers in order to get them to walk in a single line.

Sloughing - Cast off or shed.

Sternum - The breastbone.

Urethra - The duct by which urine is conveyed out of the body from the bladder and which in male vertebrates also conveys semen.

Whittle - Carve (wood) into an object by repeatedly cutting small slices from it.

www.ingramcontent.com/pod-product-compliance
Lightning Source LLC
Chambersburg PA
CBHW072133280526

45788CB00002B/621